FOREWOR

by

Lilian Watts

Shortly after I had been employed by Fitups a favourite aunt, who was without any knowledge of theatre business, enquired with innocent concern: "And how is Misfits doing, dear?" She was, I think, slightly amused by my enthusiasm for the job. The firm's name meant little to her and "Misfits" was near enough. I was able to assure her that I was still receiving my weekly wage of £2, which in those days covered the cost of travel by tram and train between Miles Platting and my home, Arden House, Astley, Cheshire, leaving a modest margin of pocket money.

In those early days there were two other full time employees. One was Charlie Spur, all five feet five inches of him, complete with pebble glasses, a "Chaplin" moustache and an apparently immovable cap: the other was a scenic artist whose status entitled him to be addressed as Mister Palliser. Other workers needed to deal with the scenery were initially employed on a casual basis. Humphrey was a skilled worker in many types of timber construction and was no mean artist. At times he would stay alone through the night working at the bench or the paint frame to complete a job.

We all worked in quite a spacious ground floor store, with double doors at one end wide enough to admit a lorry for the loading of "flats" and a variety of "props". Comparative privacy for my desk and typewriter was created by scenic flats which had once served as part of a sun-drenched Banana Grove. Actual warmth was supplied by a one-bar electric fire. An ancient gas-stove kept glue in a fluid state and boiled the water for frequent cups of tea.

All was very friendly and informal. Humphrey spent part of his time in his office at S & J Watts in Portland Street, but as the scenery business grew his periods at Oldham Road increased, as did the number of employees there.

My job continued until the end of 1928, when I became engaged to Humphrey. On January 2nd 1930 we were married at the Savoy Chapel in London and until he died so suddenly in 1946 we lived at the lovely family home, Haslington Hall near Crewe, which Humphrey had bought when he came out of the army in 1918.

In recent years I had been very anxious that the unusual history of the firm should be written and that it could only be written with authority by Percy Corry (Peter to me). In 1983, in his 90th year, he was persuaded to do it.

Early in the 1930's he had formed a close friendship with Humphrey, whose many and varied interests gradually made it impossible for him to spend the time needed to control the expanding business of Fitups. In 1936, at Humphrey's request, Peter agreed to undertake management of the business. There was an informal understanding that ultimately he could become the proprietor. However, in 1946 the private limited company of Watts & Corry was formed but details of the transfer of the business had not been settled when Humphrey died suddenly, causing some legal complications. These were resolved only by considerable co-operation between Peter, the executors and the family, for which all concerned were very grateful. The necessary capital was raised by the company and purchase of the business from the executors was arranged.

To me the story of the firm's progress, a task to which Peter has given so much time and trouble, is of intense interest, sometimes exciting, sometimes moving and usually enlivened by light-hearted comment. It is obvious that his initiative and energetic control, with the co-operation of the highly competent staff he had acquired, developed an organisation that gained an impressive reputation internationally. In the periods of war and peace the firm overcame many difficulties and not a few daunting crises. I was more than pleased to become a director of Watts & Corry Ltd in 1946 (not a very active one, I fear) and consequently was able to have some share in the firm's success. My late husband would have been very gratified to know that the initial opportunities he created had been used so effectively.

It was good that Peter had been persuaded to include his autobiographical details in the narrative. The success of the firm was so obviously the result of an ideal partnership of Watts and Corry.

Lilian Watts, widow of Humphrey, who became a director of Watts & Corry Ltd in 1946.

INTRODUCTORY

My original intention in writing this book was to record the history of Fitups, which became Watts & Corry Ltd in 1946. In that year Humphrey Watts, the founder of the firm, died suddenly and the business became my responsibility. Description of development during my period of management became unavoidably autobiographical and I decided it would be logical to incorporate a complete sketch of my own experiences from birth in 1894 until my retirement in 1965 at the age of 71. I fear I have done less than justice to Humphrey Watts, a man of sensitive charm with many interests. His modesty and my lack of intimate knowledge of, or contact with, many of those interests prevented me from discussing them with complete authority.

For many of the details I am indebted to his widow, Lilian Watts. Also, for those concerned with S & J Watts and Company I am grateful to the custodian of the archives in the Manchester Public Libraries. I have had to rely considerably on my personal memories and those of my associates. In my ninetieth year my own memory sadly lacks perfect reliability. For any resultant errors and omissions I apologise but humbly plead in extenuation that I have preserved too few relevant archives. Some years ago I destroyed a fearsome accumulation of material which could have been useful. To those who know me as Peter, I have to admit that Percy has baptismal veracity. For many years, when writing, I used the initial that served for either. The name Peter became particularly adopted by theatrical friends and it has my personal preference. However, I still respond quite easily to either name.

P Corry

PART ONE
Early Life in Progress 1894-1934

I can vaguely recall the public fuss that was made about the beginning of the 20th century. In the absence of radio broadcasting mass communication was then mercifully limited, mainly to the press. At the time I was approaching the age of six. I do not recollect any memorable comment at school about the start of what has proved to be a period of amazing discoveries and developments. There was not then any hint of the universal threats to continued human existence which are now apparent.

The fact that the Boer War was still being precariously fought in South Africa was more insistently newsworthy. I do remember publicity about Lloyd George, in the uniform of a policeman, evading the assault of a Birmingham mob after his forceful opposition to the war, luridly reported in the press.

I have official documentary evidence that I was born in Macclesfield on 15th June 1894. In adult life I was once driving through that town on the road to Leek when my mother pointed out an undistinguished row of terraced dwelling houses and informed me that I was born in one of them. They were of modest size and would have limited facilities, say two bedrooms, no bathroom, an outdoor loo in a back yard; the front door would lead directly from pavement into a small "parlour" through which one would pass into the living room and a scullery. There would be internal illumination from oil lamps and candles. I have no actual memory of the place as we moved when I was only one year old to Edgeley in Stockport.

I reckon that in the first eighteen years of my life we occupied fourteen different houses, all rather similar in size and status. I suspect that my father's restlessness was responsible. Gradually oil lamps were superseded by primitive gas-jets whose efficiency was later increased by the fitting of incandescent mantles enclosed in glass chimneys. Electrical circuitry and apparatus developed rapidly from the 19th century onwards but it was only during my youth that it was available in our household. I don't remember in which house we first had this magical source of light. It must have been in one of the newly built houses into which we moved in Cheadle Heath, probably when I was about ten years old. Gas lighting of the streets was gradually replaced by electric lights during my youth. We missed the nightly patrol of the lamplighter, who with a long pole could turn on the taps and ignite the gas jets of the street lamps.

I was the youngest of three children, the other two being sisters who, I suspect, rather spoiled me. My father was a railwayman, as were his father and also one or two of his brothers. He was something of a radical: I recollect that in most of the houses in which we lived until I was about twelve, a large portrait of Gladstone graced the wall above the mantel shelf in our living room. Our newspaper was the radical Daily News. When I bought papers myself I chose the extravagantly priced Manchester Guardian: twopence a copy! It was probably inevitable that I should become an advanced radical quite early. Also, at the age of about twelve, it became possible for me to borrow books from the Public Library. I walked into Stockport nearly every Saturday morning to collect a fresh book. My choices were exploratory, without any outstanding favourites or any parental guidance. We had a very limited collection of books in the house and purchases were rare. My elder sister Annie (later contracted to a more acceptable Anne) was a considerable reader, but as she was about five years older than I her literary tastes were rather more mature. I don't recollect that she had any appreciable interest in or influence on my reading. The younger sister, Elizabeth (two years older than I - name later abbreviated to Beth) was not so compulsive a reader. During the years of our youth her health was a little precarious, but improved as she grew older. Our family relationship was always congenial and undemonstratively friendly: I cannot remember any major conflict between the three of us. In retrospect, I judge my father to have been an intelligent man, somewhat over tense, rather remote and inclined to be irritable. My mother was more placid and restrained. She had lived in the village of Bosley and had been what I imagine was a typical country girl of her period, hard working and conscientious. My parents were less suited to each other than was desirable and there was often a kind of neutrality between them which could be somewhat emotionally disturbing at times, although there was no active conflict.

Our move from Edgeley to Cheadle Heath was, I suspect, influenced by proximity to St John's Methodist Church and the associated day school, which became a municipal elementary school while I was there. When at the age of twelve I had secured a scholarship for secondary education, I realised that the St John's School was definitely less than first class. English lessons, in particular, were quite elementary. Our family was actively non-conformist in its religious practice. We regularly attended Sunday morning chapel services and afternoon school. My father became the Sunday School Secretary but after some sort of dispute with the School Superintendent he severed his connection with St John's and we all became Congregationalists! I think the break would have been avoided if the Methodist parson of St John's had still been there. He was a friendly Welshman named Sydney Jones who had visited us often before he was moved to Stoke on Trent. We possessed a small organ and Jones had often called in just to play our organ on which he had composed one or two hymns. We were sorry to lose him. None of our family had any musical expertise.

My recollections of those early days are rather sketchy. Queen Victoria had been on the throne for over sixty years and died in 1901. I remember a neighbour calling in one evening and, as he entered, with impressive solemnity he said simply, "She's dead". Her son became Edward the Seventh at the age of 60 and preparations for his coronation were complete when it had to be postponed because of his serious illness and operation. It had been arranged that all the school children were to have a celebration "bun fight", complete with presentation mugs. It was evidently too late to cancel the affair so we had our party without the coronation, which took place later in the year without further local celebrations.

In 1902 (I was then eight years old) I went to school one morning and found that all the scholars who had arrived earlier were sitting on walls outside the school grounds, as they had decided they must have a holiday to celebrate the ending of the Boer War. Great Britain had succeeded in annexing the Transvaal and the Orange Free State in South Africa by beating the forces commanded by Kruger. The rebellion of the scholars worked and the day's holiday was reluctantly allowed. It was my first (and only) contact with a sit-down strike!

About that time the first electric tramway between Stockport centre and the Iron Bridge, which marked the boundary with Cheadle, became operative. There was great excitement when the first tram, profusely decorated with coloured electric lamps, passed our door on the main road. We all turned out to see and to cheer. From the centre of Stockport to the Rising Sun in Hazel Grove there was still a service of horse-drawn trams, which were replaced by electric trams some years later. The horses were changed at the Crown Inn in Great Moor and the service was still operating when we went to live in the area, about 1910, I think. I travelled by horse tram but not very frequently. The travel was very cheap but we were well conditioned to walking everywhere and usually thought of riding only if time saving was imperative.

We lived in five houses in Cheadle Heath. One of them was struck by lightning while we were in occupation. During the storm Beth and I were watching the "fireworks" through the window, my mother was ironing and a maiden full of clothes was in front of the fire. Suddenly there was a terrifying bang and the room was filled with floating soot which played havoc with the clean clothes and turned us all into nigger minstrels! Thereafter, for many years, we were all nervous during thunder storms: my mother would retreat into the pantry or any other windowless darkness available until the storm subsided.

In 1906, while still living in Cheadle Heath, I gained a scholarship which entitled me to secondary school education for four years at a school on Wellington Road, then named Stockport Technical School. It was changed while I was there to Stockport Municipal Secondary School and many years later, when a new building was erected in Mile End Lane, it became simply Stockport School and acquired a more elevated status.

When two of my four years at the Secondary School had expired my father had given up his railway job owing to ill health and became an insurance agent. His modest earnings had diminished somewhat and it was thought desirable that I should start to earn money. I got permission to relinquish the scholarship and, perhaps not surprisingly, I applied for a railway job. I became a junior clerk in the Goods Manager's Office of the London and North Western Railway at London Road Station (now Piccadilly) at a salary of eight shillings per week. During the first year or so I was in the office whose junior staff had to distribute the incoming mail to the various sections and then collect and despatch the outgoing mail at the end of the day. Our office adjoined the opulent sanctum of the Assistant Manager, an arrogant type who used to summon any one of us dog's bodies by an insistent push-button bell, often merely to stand with a sheet of blotting paper to dry his flamboyant signature on a pile of letters. Unlike the General Manager, who was a quiet gentlemanly type, he was an example of how not to behave in authority. He could command obedience but not respect, and was, I think, an effective warning to an obscure junior against the misuse of power. After about a year, during which I was learning to write shorthand, operate a typewriter and act as a relief attendant at the telephone switchboard, I was transferred to a separate Claims Deparment with slightly more responsibility. One of the perks was the opportunity to buy cheaply the Barker and Dobson sweets that became salvage when the bottles were broken in transit, reducing slightly the burden of the consequent claim! I don't remember any casualties from chewing broken glass! Also, for a short period I was the junior of two of us who operated a small branch office at Liverpool Road, quite adequately without direct supervision.

At that time the clerks were all men, except for a quite separate Accounts Department in Mosley Street, where there was a staff of women who were mostly book-keepers. It was decided by the Claims Department, presumably to ensure segregation of the sexes, that women should be engaged to form a typing pool operating in the Mosley Street premises. There were about six females of whom I was put in charge, distributing the letters and assisting them in the typing when there was an excess of work. It was a job that was mildly interesting as a first experience of exercising some modest authority. The main disadvantage was that I had too little to do and began to consider changing jobs. I was then about 17 years old.

My sister Anne had been employed first in a cotton mill, then for a short time had tried nursing at a mental hospital in Cheshire (where an Aunt Dora had a surpervisory job) but Anne decided against nursing as a career. She then took a job at Faulder's Chocolate Factory in Stockport where another aunt, Jenny by name, was in charge of the canteen.

Aunt Dora was an impressive character who married one of the doctors at the hospital, and Jenny was a rather fussy spinster with a fondness for garish knick-knackery in the way of personal decoration.

Anne had developed a keen interest in the socialist movement and was also an ardent supporter of the militant suffragettes under the leadership of Mrs Pankhurst and her daughter Christabel. She persuaded me to attend meetings at the Stockport Labour Church. On Sunday evenings prominent Socialists, members of the Labour Party and a varied selection of speakers with cultural convictions addressed large audiences in the Central Hall in Hillgate with differing degrees of rhetorical expertise. The audiences were conglomerates of professional "intellectuals", lower middle-class clerical workers, minor radical shopkeepers and the like, convinced of the need to do something to remove the glaring irregularities of society. Many of them (including us) became regular readers of The Clarion, a weekly paper edited by Robert Blatchford, and were devotees of Shaw, Ibsen, Dickens and contemporary writers and reformers. There were Clarion Cycling Clubs. In Handforth there was a Clarion Club House with a tennis court and other recreational facilities; we joined and spent many happy days there, establishing congenial friendships. It was then I developed a fondness for camping together with a friend, Fred Barlow. We jointly bought a lightweight camping outfit which we could carry on our two cycles. For several years we attended Easter national conferences of Clarion devotees at such places as Shrewsbury, Buxton and Stratford. In 1914 Barlow and I had a camping holiday in Brittany and the Channel Islands, my first venture abroad. As we sailed home to Southampton we passed the massed fleet at Spithead. It did not disperse before the war began.

At the Central Hall a number of us formed a dramatic society, the Stockport Clarion Players, of which I was the secretary. Our first production was Ibsen's "A Doll's House". One of the members, Marion Smith, was a very accomplished actress and played the lead. Our producer was her father, R J Smith, who was also a founder member of the Stockport Garrick Society. Marion Smith later married Herbert Prentice of Marple, who ultimately became the producer at the Birmingham Repertory Theatre.

In 1910 Anne decided to emigrate to Australia, being one of a considerable party of females whose passages were subsidised by the Government which was anxious to assist in the population of the colony! I think she had only to pay a fare of about £12. As I was then employed by the L & N W Railway Company I could have a free pass to London and I saw the party off at Tilbury. Anne married in Australia and acquired a family of four. I saw them and their children in 1963 when I included Australia in a world tour.

King Edward the Seventh died in 1910 and was succeeded by his son, who became George the Fifth. I have no recollections of any connected events: at the age of 16, I was not entitled to municipal presentation mugs or bun fights!

When with the Clarion Players I played the lead in a play written by Ross Hills, a prominent member of the Garrick Society, and in 1912 he invited me to become part of the crowd scene in Galsworthy's "Strife", which the Garrick presented at the Theatre Royal, produced by Charles Charrington. It was an interesting and useful experience, as although I had little to do I was able to observe at close quarters Charrington's method of dealing with stage crowds. He divided them into identical groups of seven or eight of the strikers and gave them lines to say and shout appropriate to the emotions he wanted to express. As everybody spoke more or less simultaneously the actual words were indistinguishable but collectively created a realistic effect. It was this method I adopted successfully many times when I came to direct theatrical crowd scenes. It was also a technique that I was able to adapt to smaller groups of onlookers in less crowded scenes.

In 1912 I responded to an advertisement issued by the Co-operative Wholesale Society and obtained a clerical job at the Balloon Street headquarters in Manchester. As a result of Lloyd George's National Insurance Act of 1911, what were known as Approved Societies were created by insurance and other companies and were appointed to operate the scheme. One Robert Smith, a prominent member of the Co-operative movement, had persuaded the C.W.S to form such a society, which was approved and operated with the local co-operative retail societies acting as agents. It functioned as the National Insurance Section of the C.W.S with Smith as Manager. I became one of about ten men who formed the Correspondence Department. On the whole I found it a more congenial atmosphere and made many good friends. We were encouraged to join a newly formed organisation known as the Faculty of Insurance and take their examination; as a result I obtained the degree of Associate. The right to add A.F.I to my name I thought amusing rather than flattering, as it didn't provoke any advance in salary. It satisfied Smith who, without examination, had been appointed a Fellow of the Faculty (F.F.I)!

I was with this section when, in 1914, war was declared. Smith was, I think, something of a pacifist and resented enlistment of any of his staff. Nevertheless several of us decided to volunteer for service with the 6th Territorial Battalion of the Manchester Regiment. As recruits were then still accepted only by pre-war requirements I was rejected because of "Defective Vision". (Casualties soon determined that the wearing of spectacles did not bar a recruit from becoming gun-fodder.) My own rejection was fortunate for me: most of my volunteer companions perished in the futile effort to dislodge the enemy from the Dardanelles in 1915. I had mixed feelings about the whole of the war and as the dreadful slaughter increased the early appeal of

Caricature of author playing Peter Simple in Merry Wives of Windsor in 1916

adventure was dissipated and I made no further attempt to enlist. When conscription was introduced in 1916 all of us who were of military age were summoned for examination and classified for various forms of service. The top grade was A1, followed by B1, 2 and 3 and the least suitable personnel were classified as C3. I was graded B2 and awaited call-up which, in my case, was late in 1916. In the meantime, female clerks had been introduced into the office and I acquired some supervisory responsibilities. Included in the feminine recruits was a girl named Dorothy Kibble and after she had recovered from an active dislike of me, we became good friends. Had she not been engaged to a very nice man who was already in the army, our association might have developed quite seriously.

Shortly before the war my mother and father separated. My sister Beth and I joined mother and rented a small house together in Edgeley. Beth was employed by a man named Ellis who manufactured chocolate in Stockport and our joint salaries were adequate for our support. Ellis was a Quaker and was called up for non-combatant service. While he was away Beth had to run the firm with the aid of a sales agent who was able in a period of scarcity to sell all they could manufacture. Beth formed a lasting friendship with Mrs Ellis during this period. Between 1914 and 1916 I continued my cycling and camping activities and did some amateur acting. Early in 1916 I was asked to take part in the Stockport Garrick Society's production of "The Merry Wives of Windsor" at the Theatre Royal, as a result of which I joined the Society and played one other part in their own premises in Wellington Street just before my call-up.

Enlistment

In the autumn of 1916 I received official instructions to report to the army authorities in Chester for enlistment. I had learned that as a category B2 man I should probably be qualified for enlistment in the Army Service Corps and at Chester I expressed a preference for the Horse Transport Section. To my surprise I was accepted and ordered to report to the A.S.C depot in Woolwich, although apart from being able to recognise one end of a horse from the other my knowledge of such animals was negligible. In discussion with a fellow recruit in the train to Euston I discovered he had been refused a posting to the Horse Transport Section, although he was a farm worker and knew a lot about horses. It should have been obvious to the meanest of intelligence that he was a much better bet than I. It was a curious early experience of the ways in which the Army could behave. I arrived at Euston Station late on a Saturday evening and got a bed at the YMCA hut, where I decided to stay until the Monday morning as I deduced that I was unlikely to be received with any enthusiasm on the Sunday, which proved to be correct. I was complimented on delaying my arrival!

It was a chastening experience to become an anonymous unit in an unremarkable assembly of conscripts. For the first few days we did little but gradually learn the ways of soldier behaviour and how to "dodge the column"! We were issued with our uniforms and essential kit. My uniform was only partly new: the rest was more or less obviously part worn, some of it bearing evidence of having been in battle! By dint of occasional visits to the regimental tailor, exercising a little ingenuity and greasing some palms, I managed to change many of the articles of clothing and acquire some semblance of a military appearance. New riding breeches and jangling spurs were helpful.

After a few days of elementary drilling and very little else likely to be useful, a crowd of us in varied "marching order" were assembled and, led by a band, proceeded to Blackheath camp a few miles distant, where we were allocated to definite training companies with our own officers and N.C.Os. We began to lose something of our anonymity and to feel that we belonged to a unit. We were a very mixed bunch and I cannot remember having established any association of significance. We spent our days doing stable duties, foot drill with an irascible Welsh sergeant issuing commands, occasional riding instruction and learning to bump the saddle every "alternative step of the 'orse", to quote the instructor's behest. Occasionally we were taken on a troop exercise through the environs of Blackheath. On one occasion the horse I was "riding" was a rather self-opinionated beast who obviously realised he had an uncertain bloke holding the reins and bolted out of line, whereat the instructor swapped horses with me to ensure our safe and more orderly progress.

After a few weeks of training a party of us were put on draft. Rumour had it first that we were to be shipped overseas, then Buxton was stated to be our destination, but my satisfaction at the prospect of being within 20 miles of home was short-lived. In fact we moved to Brocton, which was a camp on Cannock Chase near Stafford. There we found ourselves posted to the 240th Company A.S.C Horse Transport Section. Two horses were allocated to me. At 6.00am each day we had to groom, feed and water the animals and after breakfast the horses had to be harnessed to G.S wagons, parading at 9.00am to be detailed to various jobs in the camp. There was an extensive assembly of infantry units which included a considerable number of New Zealanders and our job was to keep them supplied with rations, various commodities and equipment. There was an appreciable population of W.A.A.Cs who acted as cooks, kitchen staff, clerks and messengers and provided "human interest" for the troops, especially the New Zealand contingent who were more highly paid! The hilly roads in the camp and surroundings became very treacherous during frosty weather and the farriers had to insert nails with sharpened heads in the horses' hooves to improve their grip on the road surfaces. Sunday mornings were spent cleaning the harnesses, a less than congenial job during an icy winter. We were reasonably accommodated in wooden huts and were fed quite adequately. As a result of the life in the open, with regular exercise inducing a healthy appetite, I put on some weight and was very fit.

After being at Brocton for a couple of months or so, I and a few others were transferred to a small detachment of the same Company operating at Lichfield, supplying all the necessary transport for a barracks, an Officers' Training Company and a hospital. The detachment was about twenty strong in the charge of a sergeant with a couple of corporals and a man acting as clerk. Quite a pleasant cosy family, occupying what had been part of the peacetime married quarters. I was given a pair of mules (we hadn't any horses), one of which had acquired the knack of slipping its halter and leaving the open stables at dawn for the adjoining racecourse. After a futile endeavour to catch the mule on the first morning, I found it was only when we created the noise of emptying the feed tins into the mangers that my mule would return for breakfast voluntarily. As we found it impossible to prevent the slipping of the halter, that became standard procedure.

It was quite a happy life but after a few weeks the man who was doing the clerical work of the detachment was ordered back to Company headquarters for transfer to the infantry. The sergeant was evidently convinced that I could be mightier with the pen than with the driving reins and I was deputed (nothing loath) to undertake the simple office work. In practice I found that my predecessor had simplified simplicity and the job had been discharged with something less than expertise!

I soon found it possible to clean things up and to organise the work rather more efficiently, with everything running smoothly. Then we received instructions that I was to be transferred to a much larger detachment of the Company at Rugeley Camp only a few miles from the Brocton headquarters on Cannock Chase. I reluctantly left the cosy billet in Lichfield and reported to a Captain Yates, who was in charge of the Rugeley detachment. This was a much larger outfit, consisting of a field bakery section, a butchery department and a large grocery store as well as the horse transport group, catering for the needs of the entire camp in which infantry units were housed. There was very little motor transport. The Captain was a pleasing personality who welcomed me the more warmly because I was, nominally at least, a driver of horses. He had been told I was an experienced orderly room clerk, about which I disabused him, but he remained quite cheerful. He told me the office was in a hell of a mess and I could have a free hand to do whatever I thought necessary to get it into some order. I soon found his diagnosis was deplorably understated. There wasn't even a nominal roll of the personnel attached to the various sections of the unit! For the first few weeks I worked until late every evening when creating order out of the chaos. Very shortly the Captain was posted elsewhere and he was replaced by a Lieutenant J A Cochran, who was a brother of C B Cochran, the celebrated theatrical entrepreneur. He was a delightful man and easy to work with and we established a very pleasant and friendly relationship. After a few weeks Cochran suggested it was all wrong that I had no stripes to indicate the quite considerable authority I had to exert. I said that any less than three stripes would be useless, but the rate of pay was not important, as any increase in Army pay would be deducted from the allowance from the C.W.S which made up the Army pay to the equivalent of my salary when I joined the forces.

Promotion

After visiting the Major in command of the entire company I was informed that I would be officially promoted to the formal paid rank of Corporal, to be followed immediately by being given the rank of Lance Sergeant. My sleeve acquired the three stripes and I was able to move into the Sergeants' Mess, which was a great improvement in my living conditions. My work was unaltered except for occasional duties as Orderly Sergeant. I was able to arrange for one of the drivers to be transferred to my office as an assistant. He was an intelligent young man named Shelton and he soon settled in very amicably. His parents lived in Wolverhampton and we frequently visited them together. I arranged to transfer my cycle from home to the camp. It was most useful and enabled me to see a lot of the very attractive surrounding country as well as being useful about the camp. Occasionally I was able to borrow a horse from our stables and rode across the moors on my visits to headquarters at Brocton.

There was a Garrison Theatre at the Rugeley Camp to provide entertainment for the troops. One of the infantry officers, Reggie Sharland, often performed with his wife, Annie Croft, a well known musical comedy artiste. Another popular performer was an attractive amateur living at Hednesford named Gladys Stanley, who, after the war, became a professional actress who then started to spell her name "Gwladys". She was a popular Principal Boy in pantomime and ultimately married Francis Laidler, a prominent producer of pantomimes in Leeds. Many years later, as Chairman of the Manchester Branch of the Society for Theatre Research, I organised a Pantomime Exhibition and the ex Principal Boy performed the opening ceremony attended by stars from the local pantomimes. As my duties at Rugeley did not allow me enough spare time to join the nucleus of the Theatre Company I did not establish any direct concern with the theatre but, with the approval of Lieutenant Cochran, I did organise a few concerts for our detachment's personnel and appeared on stage occasionally to recite a few of the more dramatic and sentimental "selections" popular with the troops!

On the whole my life at Rugeley was pleasant. I was busily and usefully occupied. The environment could be rough in the winter but during the rest of the year the countryside was most attractive. I was able to obtain for my mother and Beth comfortable holiday accommodation in an attractive farmhouse near the camp.

Transfer to Headquarters

Late in 1917, much to my regret, I was transferred to Company Headquarters at the Brocton camp to act as assistant to the Company Quartermaster Sergeant. The Commanding Officer was a Major St Clair, a regular soldier and a very popular officer. My immediate officer was a Captain Goddard, with whom I was able to form a good relationship. Our Orderly Room was supervised by a Regimental Sergeant Major, a Jewish cockney named Sam Isaacs who, after retirement from the regular army, had owned a chain of eating houses (possibly chip shops) in London. He professed to have a profound contempt for the "Kitchener's Army" lot, whom he regarded as amateurs without proper regard for regimental discipline. In arguing with him, I stressed the fact that the N.C.Os on whom he relied were invariably temporary soldiers and those whom he constantly chivvied were or had been regulars. My C.Q.M.S (surnamed James) was a regular serving soldier and was much bullied by Isaacs. By order of promotion James could have been a Company Sergeant Major but unfortunately for him when promotion was due the vacancy was for a C.Q.M.S (equal in rank), which he had to accept. He would have been a good C.S.M, the rank he would have preferred, but was rather a misfit as C.Q.M.S. Fortunately I was able to take over most of his clerical duties, with the assistance of a very competent W.A.A.C clerk who was not only very capable but was also pleasingly decorative. She was an intelligent worker and a North Country lass. She was much cultivated as a companion by the New Zealand troops in the Camp.

On reflection it seems to me that life with the 240th Company of the A.S.C (which became Royal Army Service Corps during my service) was reasonably comfortable and pleasant. Although we were all insignificant cogs in a vast military machine we had a placid existence quite remote from the sanguinary slaughter in France and the frightening casualties on other battlefields. We were, of course, liable to be moved to what were currently referred to as other "theatres of war", but until orders were received from authority we were little worried. On one occasion, when there had been some increase in casualties, we received instructions that all N.C.Os had to be medically examined and classified as to fitness for service in any of the theatres of war. I was surprised to be certified as unfit for service in any theatre! I was stated to be suffering from a disorderly action of the heart, which rather perturbed me but created suspicion in the absence of symptoms. I had seen my Captain leaving the Medical Officer's premises on my way to the examination. The next time I was on leave I saw my own doctor and insisted on a thorough examination, after which I told him why I needed his opinion. He dismissed the diagnosis of D.A.H and said there was merely a slight murmur which was not at all serious. I suspected there had been something of a wangle but was quite relieved not to be immediately liable for active service. I had seen more than enough of the consequences of active combat to make me pleased to avoid it. It was a warning that my congenial existence, as I had already realised, could be quite temporary.

Before I left Rugeley Lieutenant Cochran had been moved and replaced by a recently commissioned officer named Wesson, a former civil servant who had also been a warrant officer in the Territorials and with whom I became very friendly. Shortly after my transfer to Brocton my Captain was replaced by a Captain Rankin, who had been boss of a firm of flour millers in Liverpool. He was less ideal as a substitute for Captain Goddard, with whom my relations had been free and easy. With Rankin I found it tactful to emphasise my recognition of the difference in our ranks by being over-punctilious in thoroughly regimental behaviour without any human familiarity. He got the message and our relationship became consistently "correct" but quite reasonable. The C.Q.M.S and I became close friends. I think his first name was Ernest but his intimates always called him "Jimmy". The two of us shared the same living quarters and he swore he had slept very much better since I had joined him in the same room. I think the fact that I was relieving him of a lot of the work that had worried him formerly enabled him to relax and to sleep more easily. For many months we shared a pleasant association.

On 11th November 1918 we celebrated the ending of the war by sharing the universal junketing by the troops. We could look forward to resuming civilian life. I had the task then of arranging for our personnel to be demobilised. In the early days of the demobilisation process there were issued what were known as "priority slips" - authority for early release of personnel who had been nominated by their former employers. R.S.M Isaacs was rather caustic when authority for my early release was not received. It was, in fact, received the day after we had been notified by Army Council Instruction that in future the priority slips were to be ignored. Isaacs chortled about this but I offered to wager that I could get round the instruction. He was a cautious man and refused to bet. I wrote to a man at Northern Command with whom I'd had some pleasant contact and asked him for a copy of the A.C.I providing for exceptions: I knew there would be one! By return I received a copy stating that the senior officer in command could authorise exceptions. Through my own C.O I arranged to parade before a Colonel of Northern Command, whose authority was required. My C.O told the Colonel he would be sorry to lose me but didn't wish to object to my release, which was formally authorised. I enjoyed being able to taunt Sam Isaacs! In due course I had the satisfaction of preparing my own documents and made sure I could conclude my service in Manchester instead of Chester. In many ways I was sorry to leave the unit but realised it was important to get back to civilian life in preparation for the future.

After ceasing to be an anonymous "rookie" and acquiring responsibilities in the 240th Company R.A.S.C in its detachments and at headquarters, I found life very congenial. My expertise as a horseman was rather limited. At Brocton, the Company had a comparatively small section of motor transport with which I had only restricted contact. On the whole I am sure that such ability as I possessed was intelligently deployed and I was satisfied that I was doing a reasonably good job. My associates, in all the various ranks, were an interesting cross section of society with whom I was able to establish satisfying relationships. It was, in many ways, an invaluable experience of life, enabling me to adjust easily to the niceties of discipline without protest and, I hope, without any abuse of limited authority. I was often mindful and sometimes observant of Shakespeare's assertion about the antics of "man dressed in a little brief authority".

Again a Civilian

On demobilisation I was entitled to an absurdly small allowance for the purchase of civilian clothes and a period of paid leave. Fortunately the "civvies" I had discarded still fitted me and I didn't trouble to take any holiday. I rejoined the C.W.S office staff at once. It was good to renew contact with old colleagues but sad to miss the friends who had failed to return, particularly those with whom I had volunteered for the 6th Manchesters, whose mortal remains were in the Dardanelles and elsewhere. I rejoined the National Insurance section. During our absence the rate of our salaries had remained unaltered and the increases paid when we returned were considerably less than generous. As a result all our ex-service men were rebellious and at their request I composed a "round-robin" letter to the directors. They then cancelled the decisions that had been made by Smith, our Manager, and our salaries were raised to a more satisfactory level, reasonably near to what they would have been if our service to the firm had not been interrupted. Quite understandably there was a close relationship between those of us who had served in the forces. About half a dozen of us became a party, spending each weekend in the summer camping near to Rudyard Lake. Most of us cycled there but

17

Shavian discussion between Don Juan, the statue of Don Gonzalez and Lucifer (Man & Superman, Act 3)

King Magnus trying to avoid the crises provoked by his ministers (The Apple Cart, Act 1)

Stockport Garrick Society's premises when acquired in 1920

Shaw's prophet of doom (Captain Shotover) in Heartbreak House

a couple had become proud possessors of motor cycles, then still a novelty. In the winter we forsook the tents and stayed in the farmhouse. Returning one Sunday evening, nearing Handforth, my steering became erratic and I suddenly crashed to the road where I badly gashed my chin. The steering column had broken at the head. My friends stopped a passing taxi to drive me to the nearest doctor in Cheadle, who sewed up my gashed chin. Curiously enough, the driver (and owner) of the taxi proved to be a man who had been a sergeant in the M.T section of my old 240th Company R.A.S.C at Brocton and we shared the same mess. I never saw him again after his taxi-ambulance service.

Post-war Amateur Theatre Activity

My return to civilian life enabled me to become an active member of the Stockport Garrick Society, both on-stage and off. I acted in many plays and for several years served on the Executive and the Plays Selection Committee.

During the war the Society had continued to operate, rather precariously owing to the scarcity of members, but quite creditably. There had been much discussion about the possibility of finding more commodious premises for future development. In 1919, owing to the enthusiastic devotion of Geoffrey Whitworth, the British Drama League was formed with Granville Barker as its Chairman. The Garrick Society was one of the earliest members of the League in 1920. The League was very active in promoting the establishment of amateur Little Theatres. The Garrick formed a limited company (later to become a Trust) to acquire a disused warehouse in Wellington Road, Stockport, and after extensive alterations it became a Little Theatre with a seating capacity of about 300. For many years it was known as the Garrick Hall and had a modestly equipped stage. With some aid from the Drama League it was possible to obtain a small subsidy but progress was largely due to the enthusiastic efforts of the members. The standard of productions was extremely high and the total of membership had to be restricted.

Geoffrey Whitworth also became a vigorous advocate for the erection of a National Theatre, but it was not until 1951 that he was able to witness the laying of a Foundation Stone on the South Bank of the Thames. Unfortunately he died shortly afterwards and never saw the completed building. He was a modest man who received too little credit for his efforts to ensure communal support for the theatre and for the operations of the Arts Council.

Changes of Jobs

Within a year of my return to the C.W.S I began to realise that the prospects were less favourable than I wanted and my actual job was nothing like so satisfying as what I had been doing in the Army. I began to consider alternatives. Ellis, who owned the chocolate factory where Beth was working, had formed a limited company and built a new factory with the profits made during the war. He offered me a job as salesman, travelling the North of England and the Midlands. Had I known more about the business I should have realised that the prospects were very dubious, but I didn't and decided to try it about the end of 1920. Within a couple of years the firm went bust so Beth and I were both out of a job. Along with another representative, Fred Clarke, who had been working the South Wales area, we opened a shop in Shaw Heath, Stockport, selling freshly made chocolates which Beth manufactured on the premises. Mother, Beth and I took up residence in the shop. Sales were reasonable but not sufficiently profitable to keep us. In response to an advertisement I was appointed salesman on a salary and commission basis for a Manchester firm who manufactured a little known domestic soap at a factory in Radcliffe. Anybody who has had to sell unknown soap in competition with Lever Brothers and Crosfields, or chocolates not made by somebody like Cadbury, has experienced a discouraging apprenticeship! I discovered one way round the soap problem. A wholesaler in the Potteries was interested in having his own named soap and was prepared to give away free towels to the purchasers. When I offered to get the soap packed in his own cartons and to purchase the towels in Manchester, he was willing to buy the soap by the ton. It was quite a success and having put the idea to other wholesalers in Birmingham, Wolverhampton and elsewhere I was able to let their travellers working the small retail shops in the areas sell the soap and ensure a respectable turnover for me. At the same time I had negotiated with a manufacturer of high class bottled sweets, Parkes of Birmingham, to supply our shop in Stockport and then to appoint Fred Clarke and me as Manufacturers' Agents (Corry & Clarke) selling wholesale on commission. We also secured other agencies and established quite a profitable business. We rented a showroom in the Produce Exchange building in Manchester and also attended a stand on the floor of the Exchange each Tuesday. As the confectionery agencies prospered I forsook the soap. Between us, Clarke and I covered the North of England, Wales and the Midlands.

Owning a Car

In 1926 we bought our first cars. I bought a Clyno 4-seater tourer direct from the works at Wolverhampton with the assistance of my next-door neighbour, an insurance man who did business with the Clyno firm and was able to buy on wholesale terms. I think the car cost me £112. We picked it up at the factory and I had some driving instruction on the way home. The instruction was repeated next morning, which was a Saturday, I remember. In the afternoon I took it for a run without instructor and on the Monday I left solo for North Wales on a business trip lasting four days. Obviously, I had little traffic to contend with and thereafter I was a seasoned driver, avoiding any fuss or crisis. It was possible then to enjoy driving along quiet country roads even though their surfaces were less than perfect. Happy days! The Clyno was the first of at least fourteen cars I owned until I gave up driving at the age of 80.

Marriage and Fatherhood

In the early nineteen twenties I became engaged to one of four sisters who were members of the Garrick Society, Winifred Clarke. In 1925 we were married, having bought a new semi-detached house in Garner's Lane, Davenport. Another of the sisters, Dorothy, had married Edgar Burn rather earlier, and the youngest sister,

Gertrude, married Karl Birkett a few years later. The Garrick Society proved to be something of a marriage bureau for us! Our son, Patrick, was born in March 1926. Unfortunately the doctor responsible for his delivery used forceps instead of resorting to a Caesarian birth as apparently he should have done. The forceps gripped the child's head and caused damage which resulted in Patrick being physically handicapped for life, which only became obvious when he started to walk. After a few early problems he developed into a most attractive child but we had a very worrying period when we found he was a spastic and unable to control his limbs perfectly. We consulted various specialists and a few "quacks" without any great joy. The general verdict was that we were lucky that the result of his mishandled birth had not been more serious. One of the specialists consulted was a Dr Gleeson, a G.P in Southsea who was also a part-time psychiatrist in Harley Street. He showed a keen interest in Patrick and took him to live with him in Southsea for about a month and helped my son to cope with his disability. On Gleeson's advice we sent him to Forest School, a rather unconventional boarding school in Norfolk. He was there when the 1939 war broke out and we arranged his transfer to Kingsmoor boarding school in Glossop. He benefitted from his life in the two schools but we discovered he was suffering from some spinal dislocations. Ultimately, when he was about eighteen years of age,

The author in serious contemplation and (right) juvenile Patrick Corry already interested in the art of lighting

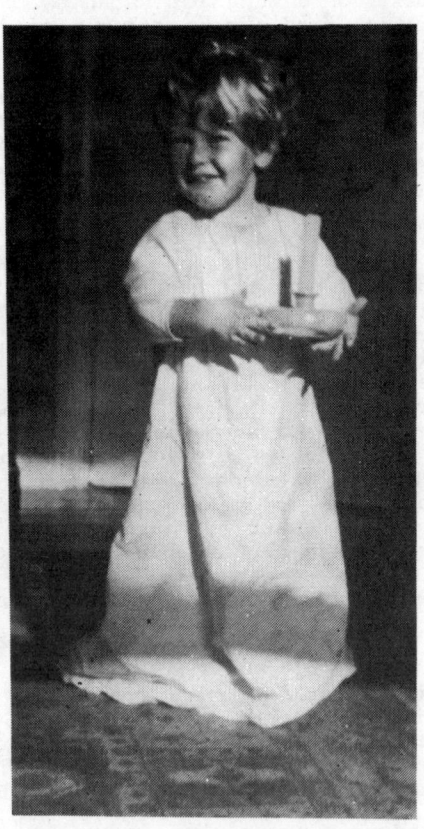

we found in Manchester a delightful and very clever osteopath named Ryan, who treated him twice a week for about six months. He was able to reduce the physical handicap considerably but could not achieve a complete cure of the damage which caused his spasticity. We were extremely grateful for the impressive improvement Ryan was able to obtain. Our distressing experience with Patrick deterred us from having any more children. Edgar and Dorothy Burn had also been unlucky. A miscarriage prevented the birth of a first child and deterred any subsequent attempt. They lived quite near to us and rather shared proprietorship of Patrick, of whom they were very fond. For many years they spent their holidays with us, mostly in Devon and Cornwall. We were grateful for their association and affectionate help.

After leaving school Patrick spent some time working with a market gardener with the intention of learning the business as a possibility for future activity. However, in 1950 Watts & Corry introduced a system of mechanical book-keeping and as it was a job of which Patrick was physically capable he joined the firm and became a very competent member. After a few years he taught a junior to operate the machine and assisted Joe Clarke in organising the installation of stage equipment; in this department he gradually became a capable and responsible supervisor. He also joined the Stockport Garrick Society and became proficient in stage management, including lighting control. He coped quite remarkably in spite of his physical limitations.

S & J Watts & Company warehouse, Portland Street, Manchester

PART TWO
Humphrey Watts - Founder of Fitups

I first met Humphrey Watts in the early nineteen-thirties when I was directing plays for the Wilmslow Green Room Society. His firm supplied scenery and stage equipment to amateur societies and the Green Room was one of his customers. There proved to be a community of interests between us but I never suspected at that time that our association would ultimately change the entire pattern of my life.

Watts had formed the firm in 1927, more as a hobby than as a commercial venture. He had named his company Fitups, which was a theatrical term usually applied to the temporary rigging of stages for performances in premises not adequately equipped for the purpose.

In fact, he was a senior partner in the prosperous family firm of S & J Watts & Company, wholesale merchants operating in an impressive warehouse in Portland Street, Manchester. Fitups was not at all connected with S & J Watts and was probably regarded by James Watts, the eldest brother and principal of the firm, as a personal whimsy to be disapproved of but tolerated as being characteristic of Humphrey "doing his own thing", in addition to his many other interests. Humphrey Watts had joined the family firm after completing his education at Oxford University and had acquired responsibility for engaging and supervising staff. He was ideally qualified for this, establishing relations with people that earned their respect and even affection: many of the juniors he engaged stayed with the firm for the rest of their working lives and became responsible and reliable seniors. When I joined him, although his capital remained in the business, he had ceased to have an active concern with the administration.

While at Brasenose College, Oxford, Humphrey Watts had joined the O.T.C and afterwards became an enthusiastic officer in the Territorial Army, in which he served for over forty years. When in camp at Aberystwyth in 1912 he had evidently taken on the messing responsibilities, as he received a silver bell which is engraved, "From the officers and men of the 5th Battalion, Cheshire Regiment to the Chef. August 1912." The 4th and 5th Battalions ultimately amalgamated and he became the Commanding Officer. He served in France with the Cheshires in the 1914/18 war.

The firm of S & J Watts was formed in 1798 by John Watts, a farmer in Burnage who also manufactured gingham cloth. When his brother Samuel joined him, they concentrated on a retail business in Deansgate and adopted their initials, S and J, in naming the company. Later they were joined by another brother, James, a name which appears to have been established as a traditional family necessity. The senior partner seems later always to have been a James. A principal partner was Sir James Watts, who was Mayor of Manchester from 1855 to 1857 and its High Sheriff. When the company forsook the retail business and became wholesalers, Sir

James was responsible for the building of their impressive warehouse in Portland Street at a cost of £100,000, a substantial sum in those days. Its facade was notable for a unique multiplicity of architectural styles, as a result of which the building was Grade Two listed in 1981.

Sir James also built Abney Hall in Cheadle in 1847. Standing in 13 acres, it was the family home for over one hundred years. One of the early guests at Abney Hall was the Prince Consort in 1857: Agatha Christie was a frequent visitor. Abney Hall became the Cheadle Town Hall in 1958.

The father of Humphrey Watts, also a James, was keenly interested in country houses and had co-operated with a Mr Fletcher Moss of Didsbury in producing a seven volume survey, "Pilgrimages to Old Houses", published by the Stationery Department of S & J Watts over a period of twenty years from 1901. In their journeys they had discovered Haslington Hall near Crewe, a sixteenth century manor house, originally a structure of wattle and daub, which had survived the ravages of the centuries. The Hall and its grounds were for sale and when Humphrey returned from the war in 1919 he was persuaded by his father to buy the place. During the alterations he thought necessary he discovered that some of the precious oak panelling had been dismantled and used to provide white-washed stalls for cattle in the shippon! At the risk of provoking bovine resentment, the partitions were restored to their former domestic glory.

Haslington Hall was the home of Humphrey Watts until he died in 1946. He was a man of many parts and very varied activities. During his early days at Haslington he created a successful unit for breeding poultry for exhibition. He engaged Michael Harrison to take charge of the unit and they exhibited at the Crystal Palace and other premier shows, both becoming expert breeders and judges. In 1939, however, the exhibition poultry had to yield priority to the more essential utility poultry.

Humphrey Watts became President of the Poultry Club of Great Britain and in due course was made Honorary Member which, it was officially stated, was the "sole award within the power of the Club's Council to bestow for his work on behalf of the poultry industry."

During his lengthy service with the Territorial Army he assumed command of the 4th/5th Battalion of the Cheshires, a post which he relinquished in 1930 and was appointed Honorary Colonel of the regiment, an honour normally reserved for a royal recipient. His immediate predecessor was the Prince of Wales, who fleetingly became King Edward the Eighth.

Among the responsibilities he accepted at various times were those of:
    Director of the British Red Cross Society in the County of Cheshire.
    Welfare Officer, Western Command
    President of Cheadle and of Haslington Branches of the British Legion
    A ranker in the Haslington Home Guard

Although in civilian life he was, when I first knew him, usually

referred to as "the Colonel", to the employees of Fitups he was always "the Guvnor", the customary title given to the boss in the theatre business.

For many years he was an active member of the Manchester Amateur Dramatic Society, for whom he acted in and/or produced many plays which were staged at the Midland Theatre (attached to the hotel of that name) and, after that theatre had closed, at the Altrincham Garrick Theatre. He also organised, directed and acted in plays and pantomimes staged in the Crewe area. He had a fondness for the Aldwych farces and was no mean performer of the Ralph Lynn characters. He also produced more ambitious shows such as Priestley's "The Good Companions" and Coward's "Cavalcade". He was not only a very competent performer but had experience in the practical problems of staging and lighting. For many of his productions he had to rely on hiring scenery and lighting equipment and it was probably the limited choice of scenery available that provoked him to create his own firm to make what he wanted. He was a competent amateur joiner (trained as a boy by the village carpenter in Cheadle) and scenic artist, skills which earned the respect of those workers whose crafts he had to supervise. He first obtained temporary premises for the manufacture and storage of stock for hire, but soon discovered there was a growing demand for his scenery.

Humphrey Watts displaying a prize bird to ballet dancers Anton Dolin and Alicia Markova. Inset is the masked face of Diana Gould, later the wife of Yehudi Menuhin, the celebrated violinist

At that time the professional theatre in the provinces was in a period of dismal decline, owing to competition from the more comfortable cinemas, but the amateur theatre was growing in popularity. The whole technique of playwriting and production had undergone a radical change. The pseudo-romantic, the melodramatic and absurd sentimentalities had been discredited by "realistic" drama. The flamboyant attitudinising technique of acting had been replaced by more credible suggestion of reality. This made it easier for the amateur of limited ability, provided he could deliver his lines with reasonable audibility and could avoid catastrophic clumsiness as he moved about the stage, to be deluded into thinking he was acting ..... and getting away with it! There were, however, quite a lot of amateur actors with considerable ability. Many of the amateur societies relied on hiring suitable scenery and lighting and this was particularly so with the operatic societies. In the early days their choice of productions was limited; most would tackle the Gilbert & Sullivan repertoire and the scenery contractors would stock tolerable settings. Gradually the choice widened to include "The Student Prince", "New Moon", "The Desert Song", "Rose Marie", etc. Later, of course, "Annie Get Your Gun" and "My Fair Lady" were popular. As the number of shows available increased, the choice was considerably influenced by the scenery available. Before the scenic contractors could decide which shows could justify the considerable cost of providing the settings, they had to be convinced that there would be sufficient demand. Obviously there was a need for some co-operation. Most of the operatic societies were members of N.O.D.A (National Operatic & Dramatic Association) which circulated details of shows released for amateur production and other useful information. Area and national conferences provided opportunities for useful exchange of ideas and pleasant social activities and the scenery and costume contractors invariably attended. There was much friendly co-operation with these contractors both socially and through their own T.T.A (Theatrical Traders' Association), with mutual benefit.

The societies exclusively concerned with play production were less specifically catered for. Scenery stocks were less related to particular plays and if hired settings were necessary, what was available was likely to vary in degrees of unsuitability! If the need was for an oak-panelled interior it was normally possible to obtain something approximately credible, but at times the compromises available could be daunting. I remember producing a play which required an exterior set representing a scene in Holland. At the dress rehearsal I was dismayed to find a backcloth which purported to represent a Venetian scene (probably painted originally for "The Gondoliers"!) At any rate it had a canal, mercifully without the Bridge of Sighs. Fortunately, by a little adroit manipulating of the lighting, it was possible to avoid emphasising the incongruity. Many of the play producing societies devised their own scenery or relied on neutral curtains to suggest their required interiors. The scenic contractors had to rely considerably on the popular musical shows to preserve their solvency.

When I first became acquainted with Fitups, in the early nineteen-thirties, it was as a customer. Several of the dramatic societies for whom I produced plays hired their scenery. By that time the temporary premises had been vacated and a block of rather derelict houses in Oldham Road, Miles Platting, had been purchased. After partial demolition, new premises had been erected on a corner site consisting of a 20ft high scenery store with paint frame, leading to a structure at the rear with rather primitive workshop and storage facilities. Adjoining the new store was a building which could, if found necessary later, be converted very simply into corner shop premises with living accommodation. This was occupied by one of the employees, and consisted of a living room, bathroom and two bedrooms, a quite attractive unit. At ground floor level was a passage leading from the "shop" (used as an office) into the rear store. Extension of the business made additional space necessary: this provided a more spacious joiners' workshop. Additional storage space for stage lighting and other equipment was obtained in premises nearby.

Watts and I shared many interests and developed an easy and congenial relationship. On one occasion we acted together in a revue staged by the Wilmslow Green Room Society and often I would call at the Oldham Road premises to see him for a general natter. On one visit he informed me that he had become acquainted with Bertini, the band leader at the Blackpool Tower Ballroom, who had acquired some reputation as a result of his broadcasting on the Home Service. Bertini had asked him to share in a musical publishing venture and Watts asked me to accompany him on a visit to Blackpool. Neither of us knew much about the music publishing racket. Although we vaguely agreed to associate, there was very limited progress in that direction but there were other developments. Bertini was rather over-optimistic about his popularity and had notions of profitably touring the variety theatres. At that time many of the well known bands were doing very good business in that field and after consultation with the Brand Lane Agency in Manchester, responsibility for the Bertini tour was taken over by the Colonel. When he realised that his activities were getting

Percy Corry about 1936

Humphrey Watts about 1936

beyond the normal scope of Fitups, he suggested that I might join him and take over the management of the firm. We had not previously discussed any such possibility but the suggestion was quite interesting. I had no knowledge of the firm's financial position but if it could pay me something approximate to what I was currently earning from partnership in a manufacturers' agency, I was tempted to tackle the job. It was tentatively suggested that if I could build up the business the Colonel would be willing to hand it over to me provided he retained ownership of the building. Neither of us thought it necessary to have any formal agreement. Fred Clarke, my partner in the manufacturers' agency business, did not object: as he would then be able to take over my customers and retain all commissions it was advantageous to him. We parted amicably and I took the Fitups job without discussing details of the business and its financial status. Later, I found the latter to be rather dubious. Although the firm had made encouraging progress it had consistently failed to make a final profit. This was apparently not vitally important to the Colonel who could, at any rate, offset his losses against his liability to the Inland Revenue. But it became obvious to me that I should have to make sure that the situation was remedied and that subsidy by the Colonel became unnecessary. In the autumn of 1936 at the age of 42 I began what proved to be a stimulating adventure.

From the age of sixteen I had been very active in the amateur theatre, mainly with the Stockport Garrick Society. I had also directed (and sometimes acted) for many other play-producing societies who were willing to pay for my services. My many and varied theatrical activities which have continued and broadened throughout the rest of my life are to be summarised later.

In the early stages the Colonel (who must now be referred to as "the Guvnor", of course) was much concerned with the arrangements for the Bertini tour and was content to leave me to deal with the Fitups' problems and to establish my own authority. Bertini had resigned his Blackpool job and we attended a thronged jamboree on his final night in Blackpool. He was busy forming his new band and planning his variety programme, in consultation with the Brand Lane Agency which consisted of a father and three sons. I have forgotten the father's first name: between ourselves the Guvnor and I always referred to him as "Uncle". Although he was not much older than we were, he was rather corpulent and had a mild avuncular manner. The eldest son, Harry, was to act as manager of the Bertini Company. It was decided that a period of rehearsal was necessary and it was suggested by Uncle that the Queen's Park Theatre in Manchester, which had closed, should be rented for the purpose. This was agreed and the Guvnor later decided that he would take over a longer tenancy and re-open the theatre, which was refurnished and decorated. It again operated as a variety theatre, for which popular star performers were booked for weekly runs. One of the Brand Lane sons, Derek, was installed as manager of the theatre and their agency booked the attractions. The audiences were not "attracted" in sufficient numbers to ensure profitability except, perhaps, to the Brand Lane outfit and to the performers. After a trial season the variety bookings were dropped and Tod Slaughter's company was booked for a season of their quite amusing Victorian melodrama repertoire, which included "Sweeney Todd, The Demon Barber of Fleet Street" and such like.

29

Tod was a capable but not an outstanding actor. His warm personality, however, made him popular with the audiences: his regular "impromptu" curtain speeches were more impressive than his acting. The booking was not extended as the attendances did not justify continuation of the Guvnor's subsidy and the theatre closed again. The Bertini tour was also less successful than had been hoped. To his own surprise and disappointment his popularity did not match that of such band leaders as Jack Payne, Joe Loss, Ambrose and others. The ventures were rather costly but not entirely without fun and useful experience while they lasted. Both the Guvnor and I managed to appear in some of the bills, he as a stand-up comedian and both of us in sketches. In one sketch, "Cupid Rampant", which I had written, I appeared for one week each in St Helens and at Queen's Park between a strong man act and a trick cyclist. It was interesting to have the fleeting experience of being a "professional" performer in second-rate variety theatres and occupying their gloomy dressing rooms. In spite of these interludes, my main concern was necessarily the basic progress of Fitups.

Managing Fitups 1936-1946

My arrival as manager of the firm was, I suspect, received with something less than wild enthusiasm by the existing small staff. They probably feared that a less tranquil period was in prospect. There was an office staff of two. Marjorie Robinson, nominally secretary to Humphrey Watts, functioned variously as typist, receptionist, telephonist, accountant, etc. Although she was then about thirty years old, this was her first job. She had cherished notions of becoming a professional soloist. A singer with a great fondness for German Lieder, she had been a pupil of Frank Mullings, was a close friend of Neville Cardus and his wife and regularly attended Halle Concerts at the Free Trade Hall. Reluctantly she had arrived at the painful conclusion that she was unlikely to make the grade of professional soloist and decided to change direction. She took a course of secretarial instruction with an optimistic hope that she might become secretary to somebody like Sir Thomas Beecham. Her secretarial college was presided over by a Miss Wilkinson, who concentrated on training girls for the upper strata of the market. Marjorie, hereinafter referred to as Robbie (a name which became familiar in the theatre business), found her period of instruction to be purgatorial but stuck grimly to the task of proving wrong her father's prediction that she would never make it. In due course (much to her surprise and delight) she was able to convince the Colonel that she should have the job he had to offer. Her delight was rather marred by my appearance on the scene a few weeks later. I could not compete with the Colonel's charm and the prospect of congenial calmness was rapidly dispelled. Fortunately she was able to adjust when she found that her lack of clerical experience was less important than she had feared. She was highly intelligent and soon became a capable addition to a collection of unusual characters with a common purpose. The other occupant of the office, Bill Watkins, was a typical Mancunian who had graduated from driving the firm's motor lorry to doing an imprecise variety of jobs. He had a lively sense of fun and was addicted to writing doggerel verse on the slightest provocation. It had been found to be more economical to hire transport, as needed, from a private contractor, Tommy O'Brien, who gradually became an invaluable associate of Fitups, which was his almost exclusive customer. He was practically accepted as a member of the staff.

The occupant of the flat was Charlie Spur, a former stage manager in one of the minor theatres which, like so many others, had failed to withstand the cinema's competition. He did not welcome my appearance. His job was to supervise the stores and organise the labour needed in fitting up the various shows. His relationship to "the office" was perfunctory. Subsequently he was dismissed, rather reluctantly, by the Guvnor: Charlie had abused the consideration and generosity he had received by fiddling the petty cash and not being clever enough to conceal the fact.

Another member of the staff who had been recently recruited was Christopher Mallinson, a young man who combined artistic flair with practical expertise in stage settings and the electrical intricacies of stage lighting. He was an individualist with a nice sense of humour. His precise responsibilities were hard to assess: he wandered in and out of office, workshop and stores, often in a rather vague state of contemplation. He had co-operated with the Guvnor in the preparation of a catalogue which was with the printers when I arrived. He was helpful in many ways.

The rest of the staff consisted of a couple of scenic artists, a few joiners, several "stage hands", a minor draughtsman and a few others of mixed abilities: a motley collection of contrasting characters, most of whom appeared to accept me without rancour or any particular concern.

In the early days one endeavoured to relate a rather primitive costing system to the quotations submitted to the hire customers. Not very surprisingly the prices had to be raised, provoking a mild consternation in the amateur committees involved. They had become accustomed to having their pleas of impecuniosity considered sympathetically, but were soon reconciled to more realistic estimates. Apart from the hire business there was modest activity in the equipment of stages with curtains and a variety of accessories. The catalogue in preparation was intended to stimulate that activity with both professional and amateur theatres.

Expansion Begins

One section of the catalogue listed a comprehensive range of stage equipment including safety curtains, curtain tracks, suspension gear and assorted ironmongery, manufactured by the Hall Manufacturing Company. There followed in the catalogue an even more impressive range of Strand Electric stage lighting equipment. It seemed obvious that if we were to develop the hire and sale of these companies' products it was desirable that there should be some special agency terms.

Formation of Strand Electric Branch

Both firms were approached, beginning with Strand Electric which, as the leading firm in stage lighting, had the greater potential. They were not willing to grant any special agency: they feared loss of complete control. Their objections were countered by a suggestion that a Manchester branch should be formed, I being engaged as manager at a nominal salary of £1 a week plus a share of profit to Fitups, thus ensuring that they could sack me (or I could resign) if the venture did not succeed. They were intrigued by the suggestion but not entirely convinced until I said we should go ahead with a development of the stage lighting business, either with or without them. Formation of their first branch was then agreed and I was appointed Manager on the terms suggested with Mallinson as Assistant Manager. Anticipating success of the negotiations, I had already engaged Cyril Whitter, formerly stage electrician at the Prince's Theatre, Manchester, as a salesman of stage lighting equipment. He was an amiable character, brimming with enthusiasm, and had no little responsibility for the development of the Branch which opened in the autumn of 1937.

In the meantime the Hall Company had been persuaded to accept the special agency idea. Close relationship with both firms developed rapidly and arrangements were made for Mallinson to spend a few weeks with Strand Electric in their London Headquarters. We formed pleasant relationships with various people involved and many lasting friendships were started. To one who had flirted with the idea of becoming a professional actor, it was pleasing to find that by using the name Strand Electric I could gain admission at any stage door in the country. There was a growing interest in amateur theatres. Many societies were acquiring their own Little Theatres. In association with Strand Electric we organised lectures in many parts of our area in the North and in the London demonstration theatre. In schools, colleges and universities the study and practice of drama was of growing interest and we helped quite significantly to stimulate that interest. Whitter and I toured most of the professional theatres in the area to make certain they knew of our existence and ability to provide useful co-operation.

Publication of TABS

In 1937, Hugh Cotterill, a director of Strand Electric, was made responsible for the publication of TABS, a journal which proclaimed itself to be "Issued in the interests of the Amateur Theatre". The first issue featured the newly formed Manchester Branch. It was issued free to leading amateur societies, to educational authorities and to others who were sufficiently interested to get their names on the mailing list. Editorial comment in the second issue stated "The response to the first issue of TABS has been most encouraging. Every post brings us requests from amateurs as far apart as Cornwall and Aberdeen to receive all subsequent issues". The early issues were modest in scope but circulation expanded quickly and was ultimately world wide, when the journal ceased to be concerned mainly with amateur theatre. Some of us became regular contributors, initially anonymous: by implication we spoke for Strand Electric but as the contributions became more obviously personal our names began to appear. In 1961 the Editor, Frederick Bentham, and I visited Canada and the USA to inspect new theatres and to attend an international conference. We were pleased and rather flattered when Ed Kook, president of the New York firm of Century Lighting Inc, which was broadly the American equivalent of UK Strand Electric, displayed his attractively bound collection of TABS, about which he was more than complimentary.

Extension of Premises

The additional accommodation needed for the stocks of Strand Electric and Hall's equipment was provided by extending the Oldham Road premises. The new building was connected to the older one, both at an increased height and sharing the frontage. The structure at the rear was dismantled and the added building extended to that site. An overall upper floor was created and it was possible to provide, in addition to the extra storage, a new paint frame, a joiner's spacious workshop, a room for making curtains and additional office accommodation. The staff had increased considerably to cope with the extended activities. Generally speaking we had little difficulty in recruiting people who fitted well into our community. Established employees were often able to recommend others with whom they had worked elsewhere. We had excellent relations with our local Employment Exchange Manager, who understood what type of individual was most likely to suit. He supplied several school leavers who became competent and responsible seniors in due course. On one occasion he sent two boys of 14 years of age, Ken Greaves and Herbert Hughes, as possibilities for one vacancy. Convinced that each had potential quality, I engaged both of them. Greaves ultimately became a director (and assumed managerial responsibility when I retired) and Hughes became manager of the Strand Branch.

With the dismissal of Charlie Spur the flat was vacated. The Guvnor and I had the living room and the large bedroom transformed into private offices and Robbie had a smaller bedroom: she had undertaken added duties for the Strand Branch. She now dictated her letters to recently acquired shorthand typists! Mallinson also had his own office on the new floor.

The Oldham Road premises of Watts & Corry Ltd and Strand Electric

Amalgamation with a Competitor

Early in 1939 a local firm of scenery contractors, Scenery Hire Services Ltd, lost their entire stock of scenery by fire. I invited them to consider amalgamation with Fitups, who would then transfer to a new joint company their stock of scenery, considerably reducing the stocks that would otherwise have to be replaced with the funds available from the insurance company. It was realised that the abolition of local competition would be good sense and Fitups could then concentrate on stage planning and equipment in association with the Strand Branch. A new company was formed, Scenic Studios Ltd, under the Guvnor's chairmanship, the other directors being Christopher Paling and Stanley Woodliffe of Scenery Hire Services Ltd, plus Mallinson and myself. The newcomers also brought with them a few of their key people who fitted in perfectly. Paling was a scenic artist with originality of style and a lot of theatre experience. He was able to take control of the new company, Woodliffe having the office responsibilities. During the spring and summer of 1939 Scenic Studios Ltd was firmly established. The Guvnor became keenly interested in their activities and I was then able to concentrate on the development of the Strand Branch and the stage planning and equipment activities of Fitups with the aid of Mallinson, Whitter and others. The progress was encouraging. Whitter was an energetic salesman and made many useful contacts. A notable one was with Henry Elder, a young architect who had a keen interest in theatre and cinemas. Several of his very original designs of cinemas had attracted national interest. Whitter, quite rightly, decided that Elder and I had much in common. Fitups co-operated with him on several jobs and we formed a friendship that strengthened over the years, and one that has been mutually helpful and delightful.

Crisis

During the period in which we were concerned with the problems of this development we had allowed ourselves to ignore the storm clouds gathering over Europe. The 1938 warning conveyed by the pathetic waving of Chamberlain's white flag, symbolised by that dubious scrap of paper on which Hitler had penned his promise, was forgotten. Consequently we were not well prepared for the shock when Adolf shoved his nasty spoke in our well lubricated wheel. Our well laid plans appeared to have gone sadly agley.

PART THREE
Fitups at War 1939-1946

In August 1939 the Guvnor and I were both on holiday, he in the North of Scotland, I in Cornwall. We each heard on the radio one of Hitler's belligerent outbursts and news on general mobilisation we both decided at once that a return to Manchester was necessary. Neither of us was surprised that we arrived at the office within an hour of each other a day later.

Inevitably the beginning of the war created temporary chaos. It was universally expected that there would be immediate aerial attacks with mass bombing of our towns, as had occurred in Poland. Civilian volunteer units proliferated to cope with possible emergencies and numerous enthusiasts became spare-time firemen to augment the regular services. The Red Cross Society and other local organisations increased their personnel. Home Guard Companies were formed all over the country. (Television's "Dad's Army" was an amusingly affectionate caricature.) Theatres and cinemas were closed. There were many changes of production in factories. Petrol rationing was enforced. Inevitably there was much uncertainty and improvisation in planning immediate developments.

The effect on Scenic Studios was catastrophic and the programme of work was disrupted completely. Paling's immediate reaction was to talk of rejoining the army in which he had been commissioned in the previous war. He was talked out of that as it seemed obvious that he would be needed. In general, the employees decided to wait and see what would happen. The Guvnor was asked to take on military responsibilities at the Cheshires HQ in Chester. Mallinson joined his father (a consulting engineer), whose firm of Mallinson & Eckersley were proposing to develop an engineering section. Woodliffe, who had been the working son of a Lincolnshire farmer, decided to return to rural scenery, forsaking the theatrical variety, and with Paling's aid he obtained a small farm in Cheshire. Some of the staff moved to other jobs and some were expecting to join the Forces in the near future. It seemed obvious to some of us that it would be a prolonged war but few, if any, doubted that we should win in the end.

The whole staff was assembled and assured that we should certainly find work which would require the varied skills we possessed. In the meantime we wanted their assurance that they would do whatever job we asked them to undertake, whether or not their own crafts were needed. They agreed unanimously, which was most helpful. In the early days we tackled all kinds of jobs, including creation of air-raid shelters. To satisfy the local authority we transformed our own basement into an air-raid shelter, which was much used by local inhabitants when the air-raids became a disturbing reality. We also made and installed black-out curtains in factories and offices: in addition we equipped stages in canteens etc. We managed precariously to keep staff employed while something of a more permanent and suitable nature was sought.

Camouflage work seemed to be a possibility worth exploration and I decided to approach the Air Ministry for a start. I visited London and obtained the name of somebody in the Ministry whose job involved camouflage work. By exercise of a little discreet sales bluff at the reception desk and having a quite extraordinary bit of good luck, due to a casual encounter in a corridor, I was interviewed by an architect named Chadwick, who was closely concerned with camouflage. He proved to be a Mancunian and in the course of friendly conversation we discovered we had a mutual acquaintance. Although Chadwick could not offer any hope of our securing camouflage work, after I had described our facilities and line of business, it occurred to him that there was a job which could well suit us. He took me to the office of a Flight Lieutenant MacDonald, who was involved in the initial training of recruits in the Initial Training Wings. There was under consideration a method of selection of potential pilots by use of the Link Trainer, a flight simulator imported from America, which had so far been used to instruct pilots in "blind" flying at night with the aid of instruments. Fortunately the interview with MacDonald began an activity that continued throughout the war and provided us with interesting work, dependent on adaptation of theatre techniques to the less congenial process of ensuring destructive efficiency.

Synthetic Trainers for Royal Navy and RAF Personnel

MacDonald explained that the Chief Instructor of a Flying School in Derby had experimented in selecting those recruits who could be trained to be pilots and, perhaps equally important, weeding out those who lacked the aptitude. The Link Trainer was installed in a Nissen hut, the walls of which had been crudely painted to represent scenically the various flying conditions that could present problems to a pilot. The installation was rather primitive but had proved to be worth improvement and considerable extension. Arrangements were made for us to inspect the "mock-up". Paling and I visited Derby and realised the possibilities. We were also allowed to arrange a flight over Cheshire to study the actual conditions as observed at a height of about 5,000 feet.

I was introduced to the importer of the Link Trainer, the J V W Corporation Ltd, controlled by a retired Air Commodore, one Peregrine Fellowes, whose distinguished career had at one time included a flight over the top of Mount Everest. It had been assumed that the J V W Corporation would be the main contractors for the project. A group of London scenic artists, under the leadership of a Yorkshire man, Myerscough Walker, had also been involved in early discussions. A conference at Cambridge was arranged for consideration of several alternatives. MacDonald had flown from London with his Sergeant Navigator and I accepted an invitation to fly back to Hendon as a passenger. We flew through a thunderstorm, lost our way and there was some apprehension about the presence of barrage balloons which, mercifully, we avoided. I saw Air Commodore Fellowes the following day. It was apparently assumed that we should be included in the team responsible for the development. We agreed about the alternative to be selected and I was asked to visit Hastings to inspect the premises that had been commandeered and to prepare a suggested layout. The premises selected were a cafe on the sea front and the

White Rock Pavilion, a newly erected multi-purpose hall. We agreed that the West End scenic artists should be employed and that we should provide and erect cubicles to house the Link Trainers. We thus acquired the responsibility of general organisation of the installation as sub-contractors to the J V W Corporation, with whom close co-operation was established, in addition to a constant friendly relationship with MacDonald and his associates.

The use of Synthetic Trainers was becoming popular with the services. We found that many of these were more concerned with mechanical operation than with realistic effects, which were essential in the Visual Link Trainer projects. Our own theatrical experience made it obvious that as the basic requirement of all training was to induce automatic reaction to a particular stimulus, it was essential to suggest reality as effectively as possible to enable the pupil to suspend disbelief and avoid any assumption that the training was merely concerned with learning to use a gadget. In the course of the development of subsequent trainers, now to be summarised, this fact was demonstrated effectively, occasionally in conflict with the opinions of some of the services personnel. About this time it was decided to alter the name of the firm to Fitups of Manchester, which was not any more appropriate but seemed to be less "bald" when announced to people not familiar with its theatre usage.

Visual Link Trainers

It became obvious that the J V W Corporation's staff could not undertake the detailed organisation of the planning and provision of the Trainers, although they were expert in the installation and maintenance of the Link machines. Their chief engineer was a clever Scotsman, Morgan McLeod, with whom we worked very closely. Had we not appeared on the scene at the right time it would have been necessary to appoint some other contractor, probably one of the London firms, to be the constructional sub-contractors. There was necessarily much contact with the Air Commodore, whose office was in his house at Aston Clinton where I was frequently entertained and where I established a pleasant relationship with all the staff.

It was agreed that each training unit would consist of a circular cubicle 24 feet in diameter, the Link Trainer being in the centre. The 10 feet high walls were to be painted to represent a panoramic view of varied features, as seen from an altitude of about 5,000 feet. The horizon was revealed or concealed; clear or misty at sea; hilly country; a town partially obscured by smoke; expanses of pastures; woods etc with houses, factories, churches and other features providing landmarks. The structure consisted of a wooden framework faced with hardboard. Although it was assumed that once erected the cubicles would remain permanently, I argued that it would be sensible to construct in sections similar to scenic "flats" but curved, bolted together on site so that they could be dismantled and transported elsewhere if necessary. This would enable us to manufacture the sections in our Manchester workshop, more economically. This was more satisfactory from our point of view and was providential for the Initial Training Wings. We had just completed the erection of some 36 units at Hastings when the fall of France caused a panic transfer of the Wings to Torquay. I had an urgent call to London from MacDonald. By then he had acquired an assistant, Charles Bell who, before he re-joined the RAF, had been employed by G B Kalee, concerned with the equipment of cinemas and theatres. He was a fellow member of the Illuminating Engineers Society and was a congenial addition to the team: we talked the same language. MacDonald, Bell and I made an emergency trip to Torquay and Paignton, where a large garage and a country club were commandeered. An immediate removal of the Trainers was organised and very quickly completed. Additional Trainers were also installed at Newquay, Aberystwyth, Oxford and Cambridge.

Torpedo Attack Teacher (Aircraft)

On one of my visits to Aston Clinton I was met by a depressed McLeod, who warned me that during the Commodore's absence in America the J V W Corporation had been approached by a Naval Officer on behalf of the Fleet Air Arm, who wished them to undertake the development of a Trainer for instruction of pilots of torpedo carrying aircraft. They had agreed subject to the approval of Fellowes, but on his return he was vigorously against the project, which he did not consider they were able to undertake. When he told me of his objections I argued strongly that if the Fleet Air Arm needed the Trainer he was not justified in refusing to co-operate. After much discussion Fellowes (with cunning malice aforethought, I suspect!) said he would agree only on condition that I would take responsibility for organising the project. I suspected that he had deliberately contrived to put me on the spot

Prototype Torpedo Attack Teacher for Fleet Air Arm installed at Crail, Fifeshire. (Sketch by Harry Rutherford)

but agreed, subject to his consent to my having a priority call on the services of McLeod at all times. It was then decided to go ahead with the project, much to the satisfaction of McLeod and of Alfred Whitehead, the Office Manager, who had suffered the Commodore's displeasure. The suggestion of the Fleet Air Arm was that the Link Trainer should be placed inside a circular translucent screen, outside which a truck should circulate, bearing a projector which would throw the shadow of a target ship. I thought it unlikely that sufficient realism could be suggested and arranged a meeting at the Strand Electric demonstration theatre so that alternatives might be considered by Lieutenant de Mahe, the Naval Officer who had originated the idea, and all the others who were to be concerned. We showed the front projection of a realistic object in colour on a solid screen and it was decided to proceed with experiments with front projection. There followed much "back-room" technical trial and error and numerous discussions with and demonstrations to all concerned, including RAF personnel likely to become involved.

When the overall details had been settled it was agreed that a prototype Trainer should be installed at the Fleet Air Arm station at Crail, in Fifeshire. Contact was established with what was always popularly referred to as the "Works and Bricks Department" (I have forgotten its official designation) and plans of the building they had to supply were drawn up. There was also much planning and construction to be organised in Manchester, London and elsewhere but all concerned appreciated the need for urgency. Installation was started as quickly as possible. The completed installation consisted of a solid circular cyclorama 44 feet in diameter and 23 feet high, curved inwards at top and bottom. Substantial timber formers created the basic shape. To this structure extruded metal sections were attached, concrete being applied to create the cyclorama, which was plastered to a smooth surface and painted at the lower portion to represent the sea. The upper portion was off-white to allow projection of sky effects. The Link Trainer was in the centre. A segment of the cyclorama was omitted to provide a control position. In here were the lighting control panel and a glass topped table bearing two crab recorders which traced the courses of the "aircraft" and the "target". In planning the visual effects we had resorted to theatrical lighting techniques: by the mixing of primary colours (red, green and blue) flooding the cyclorama, with still clouds (fleecy and stormy) projected, we were able to suggest a variety of sky effects (sunny day, stormy day, moonlight, dark night, sunset, etc). All lighting was controlled through a motor-driven dimmer bank, operated by a push-button selector control. Frederick Bentham of Strand Electric had devised this system, enabling it, for the first time, to be mass produced. Special lanterns, for projection of horizon effect at night, and other projections to suggest movement over the sea were designed. A complicated epidiascope projector, suspended above the Link Trainer created an image of the target ship on the cyclorama, which varied in size and inclination according to range and bearing. A brass model (100 feet to 1 inch) of a German or Japanese ship was fixed to the spindle of the projector, the rotation of which and the travel of moving lenses were controlled electrically by impulses from the crab recorders. The relative movements of the two were governed by a range bar connected to the two recorders. When the dropping of the torpedo was simulated the target was frozen and the Link could take avoiding action. When the instructor had worked out the distance the torpedo would have to travel, a line of light on the cyclorama would indicate its course. The Link was returned to the position at which the torpedo was released, the ship was re-started and allowed to travel for the exact period required for the torpedo to reach the ship's course, thus showing a hit or miss.

At first the exercise was required to start when the aircraft was on a straight and level course but as the installation proceeded it seemed to me that this was too simple to justify all the trouble and expense involved. Arrangements were made for me to see what was involved in an actual attack. The chief instructor at Crail took me in a Swordfish (affectionately known in the Fleet Air Arm as "the old string bag") on a practice attack on a ship cruising in the Firth of Forth for the purpose. Clad in a service flying suit, with parachute added, I stood behind the pilot in the open observer's cockpit. We approached the target at height, evidently to enable the pilot to decide on the angle of attack. Not being acquainted with the usual procedure, I was unprepared for the steep dive which followed and the turn preparatory to a broadside attack. The centrifugal force deposited my backside on the observer's seat and I missed the subsequent detail of the first attack. The exercise was repeated a few times. It was necessary to end the dive at a height of 50 to 100 feet above the water, to turn to face the target, fly straight and level for a distance before releasing the torpedo, then take action to avoid the inevitable gunfire. As we returned to the airfield the pilot had his bit of fun. We approached at height, then without any warning went into a steep power dive, disturbing my equilibrium somewhat. When we alighted I was told by the pilot that he was demonstrating what it was like to carry out a dive bombing exercise!

When I was able to report to the naval officers and the back-room boys, I was emphatic in my opinion that it was a serious error to begin the Trainer exercise at the stage when the aircraft was flying straight and level. I asserted that it was a waste of time and money if the dive and turn were not included, as they were basic factors in the attack. There was much opposition from the technical boys, who argued that the problems were too difficult, but after some arrogant persistence by me and a threat to recommend cancellation of the project they began seriously to consider ways and means. In due course they agreed on how the alterations could be made and all subsequent installations were planned to incorporate the dive and turn at the beginning of the exercise. The changes required were complicated but successful. It was not possible to alter the prototype, which was completed as originally designed. Great expertise had been exercised by the technical boffins, whose ingenuity received less credit, perhaps, than was due. When the completed prototype was demonstrated to an impressive selection of Royal Navy and RAF "Top Brass", one of the technicians who had worked on the job cynically remarked, "It was the touch of Earl's Court that sold it. They were so busy admiring the bloody sunsets that they couldn't appreciate all the technical complications involved".

After a period of re-design and much detailed testing of the revised equipment which simulated the dive, the improved Trainer was

Official certificate of identity issued by Royal Navy in 1941

approved and put into production. The cyclorama was now a complete circle, the control room being external and the instructor observing the progress of the exercise through a couple of portholes. This added to the realism as the absent section of the cyclorama and visibility of the control and recording apparatus had been something of a distraction to the pilot pupils.

The improved Trainers incorporating the dive were installed at numerous Fleet Air Arm and RAF Coastal Command Stations in Great Britain and overseas, involving us in considerable preliminary visits and consultations. In one period of fourteen days I found I had travelled thousands of miles and slept in thirteen different beds in hotels, railway sleeping cars and in service accommodation. After completion of the aircraft TAT prototype we became involved in design and installation of Trainers adapted to the needs of other Royal Navy services.

T.A.T. (Surface Craft)

After completion of the Crail prototype I was asked by Commander Villiers RN, who had been an observer of the project, to discuss the possibility of adapting the T.A.T to the training requirements of destroyer and MTB personnel. As we had been responsible for the organisation of the Aircraft Trainer we were being offered their main contract, which involved an interesting alteration of our relationship to J V W Corporation from whom we had to obtain the Link recording apparatus. Strand Electric also became our sub-contractors.

The Navy required us to design and manufacture a mechanical structure to represent a choice of either the bridge of a destroyer or an MTB, in lieu of the Link machine: otherwise the Trainer was to be identical, with similar visual effects. The prototype was to be erected at Greenock, which made it necessary for Paling and myself to establish contacts with all the people involved there, including a Polish captain of a destroyer of whose bridge we needed details. We also arranged to inspect an MTB sailing in the Irish Sea from Holyhead at night. Experience had taught us how important it was to have operational details.

The bridge structure had to rotate through 360° and to simulate pitch, roll and yaw. In the design and manufacture of the metal framework we collaborated with Mallinson and Eckersley, bringing Chris Mallinson back temporarily into our team. The unit was assembled in our premises and the timber work and furnishing completed. The apparatus for the destroyer was fixed first and opposite the MTB instruments etc were installed. Apart from the Bridge the rest of the Trainer's installation, lighting effects, recording apparatus, epidiascope projector, etc were similar to what was provided for the Aircraft Trainer. A considerable degree of realism was achieved. During tests at Greenock cases of seasickness occasionally added queasy discomfort, an unwelcome touch of the realism.

This version of the T.A.T was installed at many Naval Stations, including The Orkneys, Limovady, Devonport, Lee on Solent, and overseas. Cyril Whitter had been closely connected with the T.A.T contracts and was in charge of the installation in Malta. While he was there he had to make a preliminary visit to Johannesburg and

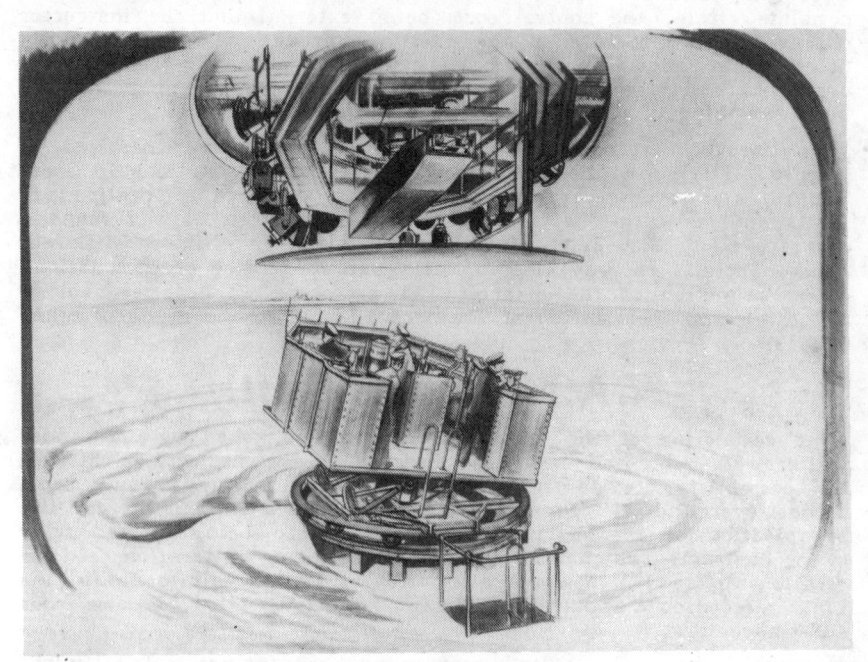

Torpedo Attack Teacher for Surface Craft personnel at Greenock (Sketch by Harry Rutherford)

in order to facilitate his travel he was able to get himself appointed an unpaid Lieutenant Commander RNVR. In his gold-braided "costume" he sailed to South Africa in a destroyer and was slightly disconcerted when he found he had been detailed as Officer of the Watch during a night sail through the Mozambique Channel. Fortunately the Germans missed a unique opportunity and our hero in fancy dress was not compelled to endanger the ship by his lack of seamanship.

On one occasion when making a visit to Devonport I was offered a bed on HMS Defiance, an old sailing ship used as Departmental HQ for training. One of our employees, Herbert Hughes, who had had experience with our T.A.T installations, had now joined the Navy and was in training on Defiance. We had a pleasant chat. Some time later we were able to arrange for Herbert to be temporarily released to assist in our T.A.T work in Manchester and Rothesay. It was, I think, a mixed blessing for Herbert, who was enjoying the service and might have stayed on in the Navy as a career.

After the war we installed this type of T.A.T in Stockholm for the Swedish Navy.

T.A.T. - Submarines

Our continued association with the Royal Navy was interestingly extended when it became necessary to study the activities of the submariners. They had decided that they wanted a similar type of Trainer for the torpedo attack. After several discussions with a Commander Teddy Woodward, a bright athletic young man of lively disposition. Paling and I visited Rothesay, where the Trainer was to be installed. It had been decided to provide it in the Portsmouth area but by the time negotiations were under way Portsmouth was liable at any time to aerial attack from France and I suggested it would be prudent to choose the Scottish site. Teddy agreed and sold the idea to his seniors. Our travel to Rothesay was less convenient, usually involving night sleepers from Manchester to Glasgow, train from Glasgow after breakfast to Wemyss Bay and ferry to Rothesay with the cattle and other assorted cargo. We became regular and warmly welcomed customers at the Glenburn Hotel. Following our now established custom we asked to be allowed to observe a practice torpedo attack in one of the submarines. Early one morning we went aboard the depot ship in the harbour for breakfast and about 9.00am joined Teddy Woodward and the crew of a submarine, Sealion, which had been on active service in the Far East. We steamed down the Clyde until we arrived off the north coast of the Isle of Arran, where we joined a cruiser which we were to attack, subsequently evading its protective destroyer. There were four junior officers under instruction in the techniques of "periscope attack": referred to, of course as "perishers". Teddy was supervising the exercise, using the second periscope. Although only an exercise it was fairly tense. Two men operated the periscopes to obey the frequent commands "Up periscope" and "Down periscope"; one man was at the wheel, two preserving the necessary level, one officer reading the scale on the periscope used for the attack, his assistant transferring the detail to what was referred to as "the fruit machine", which indicated the relative bearings of submarine and target. Another officer transferred the details to yet another,

43

who plotted both at a drawing board. By use of the spare periscope Teddy kept careful watch on the "perisher's" manoeuvres. On one "Up periscope" occasion Teddy took a quick glance, then roared the command "Down periscope!" and "Down another 20 feet quick!" and kept an anxious eye on the depth gauge. When I asked him what was happening he growled, "That bloody destroyer's coming straight for us". As we heard the thudding of an engine above us he grinned and said, "Missed us by 8 feet". When each "perisher" had completed an exercise, the submarine surfaced and we ascended the conning tower for a breath of fresh air and a welcome glimpse of the sunshine. When I saw the deck was awash I only managed to avoid being laughed at by commenting that it had been raining by timely recollecting that we had been down below! When we submerged again we provided quarry for the destroyer on a hunting exercise. As we drank tea the Captain, who exercised his grim sense of humour, pretended (I suspect) concern when he informed us that on a previous exercise a live depth charge had been dropped in error.

It was an interesting experience. The scene in the control room during the mock attack is quite dramatic with everybody's attention centred on the officer at the periscope, the only one who knows what is happening above. Unless one noted the dial of the depth gauge the fact of being submerged was forgotten. The most daunting episode was when, on arrival back at the depot ship, one had to cross from the submarine's deck on a nine inch plank, very conscious of the sheer drop to the sea.

For the Trainer we created a realistic reproduction of the complete control room with conning tower access to the upper deck. A special periscope was manufactured by Barr and Stroud. The facilities were generally similar to those needed by the surface craft personnel.

By the time the installation was complete the war had ended but the Trainer was in continuous use and for some years we made an annual service. This was the only T.A.T supplied for the submariners.

Inevitably there was some overlapping of work on the various types of the T.A.T, involving much activity in Manchester and a lot of travel in visiting the many sites. Our staff had increased considerably. Strand Electric also supplied technicians from London and we acquired a reputation as "experts" in synthetic trainers. Several other ideas were experimented with, some of which were not practicable. One which did materialise was the Operational Crew Trainer (O.C.T) to instruct in offshore gunnery spotting.

Operational Crew Trainer

This was required at the Fleet Air Arm Station in Macrihanish, near Campbeltown where a T.A.T had previously been installed. Several cubicles for observers were erected. A model of a harbour installation was built on a turntable and it was to be assumed that a ship at sea was bombarding. Explosions caused by shell-bursts were simulated and were selected by the instructor, who operated them from a push-button panel. In reality the observers would be flying in a figure eight course and the variation of view of the harbour was simulated by movement of the model turntable through appropriate degrees. The shell-burst selector panel was a mimic representation of the model and the accuracy of observation was monitored by the instructor. For night-time operation the dropping of flares was suggested by the use of small medical lamps slowly lowered from above the model. This was an ingeniously effective installation involving much electrical and mechanical co-operation between Fitups and the Research Deparment of Strand Electric, Paul Weston of the latter taking charge of the installation on site. On one occasion I visited the site with a Fleet Air Arm officer and our return flight to Glasgow was diverted to Islay to pick up an ambulance case. We had to disembark at Islay to await the return of the plane. During our wait we consulted the Met. Office and were informed that we should not be able to fly. When it was stated that my Naval friend was not piloting and we were travelling by Scottish Air Lines the reply was, "Oh that's all right. They will fly in anything", and they did. We saw the wreck of a plane near the top of one of the hills as we passed over.

Other Wartime Activities

Although our constant concern throughout the war was with the construction and installation of Synthetic Trainers our staffs were engaged in a wide variety of jobs. We obtained contracts for supplying and installing black-out curtains in factories erected for war purposes in various parts of the country. Frank McCormick was in charge of a team doing this work for a long period. We equipped stages in service camps and factory canteens and coped with limited

Operational Crew Trainer at Macrihanish (Sketch by Rutherford)

demands for hire of stock scenery and curtains, including supply to a repertory theatre in Buxton. We co-operated with Dr L du Garde Peach in running the company, whose producer was Joan Kemp Welsh and included Dandy Nicholls and Jenny Laird, the wife of John Fernald.

Ultimately we did obtain a few contracts for camouflage, one of which was for an aircraft factory outside Chester. While our men were working on the roof of the latter they were startled by the sudden appearance through low clouds of a German reconnaissance plane. The pilot was no less surprised and lost no time in seeking cloud cover again.

We provided constant service to the professional theatres in our area and to a number of special productions, one of which was a patriotic pageant at Belle Vue sponsored by the Daily Mail. Laurence Olivier and Ralph Richardson, both Naval officers, were performers and Malcolm Sargent was the musical conductor. We supplied special lighting effects and I recollect having to operate a couple of portable interlocking dimmer boards. At the lighting rehearsals I was impressed by Sargent's co-operative professionalism as a performer.

Also, throughout the war period there was considerable national interest in the probabilities of future theatre development. Many of us lectured and joined discussions in London and other parts of the country without at any time considering the possibility of our losing the war.

Haslington Hall, Cheshire - family home of Humphrey Watts

PART FOUR
Post-War Activities including Formation of Watts & Corry Ltd

With the ending of the war we had many pressing problems to face. The primary need was to complete the Government contracts and agree the financial settlements. We were also involved in discussions with Norway, Sweden, Turkey and Indonesia about the possiblity of supplying Torpedo Attack Teachers. Although the projects for Norway and Indonesia developed partially they did not fully mature. We did supply a complete Teacher for Sweden. Installation, completed in 1951, was supervised by Ken Mould, who had served in the Royal Navy and joined us after demobilisation.

When I visited Stockholm as the Teacher was nearing completion, I was impressed by his friendly relationship with the Swedish naval personnel. He was a clever enginner of the strong silent type. I was amused to learn that during a stubborn argument with one of their officers about procedure Mould quietly challenged him with the query, "Have you ever been in a torpedo attack?" and, getting a negative reply, of course, said "Well I have!" which concluded the dispute. I was staying at the same hotel as Eleanor Roosevelt and her retinue but that fact had no apparent significance for her! I noted, with critical interest, that her limousine careered through Stockholm, siren blaring with an arrogant insistence, reminiscent of Chicago films.

In September 1948 we celebrated the 21st anniversary of Fitups by giving the staff a coach picnic to Blackpool. The guests at the formal lunch included Applebee and Earnshaw, directors of Strand Electric and Henry Hall, whose summer show was staged at the Grand Theatre with our scenic and lighting assistance. Lilian Watts cut the birthday cake with the Guvnor's sword. A very pleasant celebration with an inevitable tinge of sadness. Our programme proclaimed it to be "Much Ado About Something".

Which has reminded me of a previous celebration in Manchester. In 1947 Alfred Nightingale, for many years the popular manager of the Opera House, resigned to resume managerial responsibility for the D'Oyly Carte Company at the Savoy Theatre in London. Theatre folk in Manchester co-operated in the organisation of a dinner at the Wellington Hotel: this time the programme announced: Mancunian Theatregoers present "Nightie's Off"! Fitups produced a framed illuminated address which I read to the guests:

NIGHTIE'S SOLILIQUY

To go or not to go, that is the question;
Whether 'tis wiser in the end to suffer
The grimy moisture of an urban Lancashire,
Or seek for solace in a softer clime.
And by removing, dodge the rain. To flee; to fly;
To flit; and thuswise cease to share
The smoke-pall and the thousand man-made shocks

Manchester is heir to? 'Tis a consummation
Devoutly to be wished. To seek the South;
The South.... and southerners! Ay, there's the rub,
For what we gain in losing what we leave
Must give us pause; shall we not pine
For sight and scent of Irwell's stream,
For clanging sounds of Quay Street's tardy trams,
And music of Salford's native dulcet speech;
And lack the fine effluvia of fish and chips
That nightly permeates the city's thoroughfares;
May we not find Savoy and crowded Strand
An unfamiliar country to whose bourn
The traveller, returned, a stranger is;
And we may wish we'd borne the ills we had
Than fly to others that we knew not of.
But conscience would make cowards of us all
And weaken this our recent resolution
To answer London's call with resignation;
So, since her need is great for counsels wise,
For guidance in the fairer ways of provinces
Which I have learned in many years in Manchester,
Then I must go .... emboldened by the good you bear me.
Farewell! A long farewell to County Palatine!
Your memories will always freshly live in mine.

P.C

Presented to ALFRED NIGHTINGALE,

who leaves the Manchester Opera House with the affectionate wishes of the city's theatre folk and, in particular, the artists, craftsmen and technicians of the stage, on whose behalf this profane parody is offered this twenty-seventh day of February in the year One thousand Nine hundred and Forty-seven.

Personnel

There were numerous changes in staff and alterations in the allocation of responsiblity during the first few years of the post-war period.

Chris Mallinson did not return to us. He stayed with Mallinson & Eckersley; he and his father also practised as consulting engineers. Cyril Whitter emigrated to Johannesburg, intending to develop an agency for Strand Electric either in co-operation with their existing agents, the GEC Ltd, or independently. This was apparently a rather indefinite proposal which he had discussed with Jack Sheridan, although Strand Electric were not accepting any financial liability. The scheme had some dubious aspects which he seemed to ignore with his usual optimistic impulsiveness. His job as Assistant Manager of the Manchester Branch was taken by James Templeton Wood, generally known as Woody. Some years earlier we had discussed the possibility of Woody operating as our representative in Scotland but the war intervened and he enlisted in the Navy in which he became a Lieutenant Commander RNVR, an expert in radar. Before he returned to civil life Strand Electric had appointed Stage Furnishing Ltd of Glasgow as their Scottish agents and Woody was quite pleased to accept my invitation to join us in Manchester and become Assistant Branch Manager. When with us he developed a new idea for remote control of stage lighting, using thyratron valves instead of mechanical dimmers. As a result he was transferred to London to develop this electronic system by which time Whitter had decided to forsake South Africa and was delighted to resume his old job.

Ken Greaves and Herbert Hughes returned from the Navy. The former took over responsibility for an expanded Accounts Department and later became Secretary of the Company. Herbert took charge of Strand Hire Department and ultimately had full responsibility for both Sales and Hire. Scenic Studios Ltd was not revived. Woodliffe did not return to us, continuing to be a farmer. Phil Cartlitch (ex RAF) and Ernest Lee (ex Army) took over the limited scenery hire section. Only depleted stocks of scenery were available but it was possible for the department to be expanded if thought desirable. Later, when television scenery became our concern, that capacity was invaluable. Phil transferred to that section and Ernest was responsible for the stage scenery.

Several who had been recruited during the war drifted back to their former occupations. One of these was Harry Rutherford, one of the freelance artists who was a member of the group engaged on Visual Link Trainers and then joined Fitups, undertaking a variety of non-artistic jobs. He was a versatile individual with a puckish sense of humour. To compensate for a lack of occupations demanding the use of his paint brushes, no doubt, he pandered to his artistic urge by leaving libellous caricatures of me in all sorts of unlikely places! He resumed his freelance painting in London.

Two of our pre-war valued employees, Frank McCormick and Joe Clarke, both very competent foreman joiners, who had ably accepted numerous and varied supervisory responsibilities during our wartime activities, became departmental managers. There were many others who had proved their versatility and conscientious concern. They were invaluable in preserving the quality of the greatly extended staffs we had acquired. They are too numerous to discuss and, in any case, I am having to write from the unreliable memory of impending senility: at the age of 89 I am doubtless guilty of regrettable omissions. The archives are deplorably limited.

Formation of Watts & Corry Ltd -1946

During our many discussions of future development the Guvnor and I agreed that it would be prudent to form a private limited company, in which he should be Chairman and I Managing Director: Chris Paling and Robbie were also to be Directors, each having shouldered extended responsibility in their respective activities. Chris had taken over the control of the detail of stage planning and supply of equipment, with Joe Clarke as his Assistant. Robbie had surrendered her concern with accountancy, which had become the responsibility of a greatly extended department taken over by Ken Greaves. She had to retain numerous other supervisory activities including staff organisation and a certain amount of buying and selling of accessories for both firms, became a kind of foster parent to the female and juvenile employees, undertook the organising of canteen arrangements and a host of other jobs of bewildering variety.

Apropos Accounts, it should be mentioned that in 1950 we introduced mechanical book-keeping and my son, Patrick (physically handicapped from birth), was able to learn to operate the machine effectively: after a lengthy period in the Accounts Department he was able to instruct a new clerk in operating the machine and then assisted Joe Clarke in the planning and equipment of school stages, joining Bill Watkins of the original Fitups staff, who prepared the quotations in that section.

The name Watts & Corry for the limited company was an obviously appropriate choice. The initial formalities had been completed in co-operation with our accountant but we had not discussed the allocation of shares, apart from those for which we had subscribed to form the company. When Humphrey Watts died suddenly on 15th March 1946 there were complications. The firm was still included in his legal assets, and was transferred to the Executors, chief of whom were brother James Watts and solicitor, Sir Walter Cobbett.

His death was a tragic loss to all of us.

Humphrey Watts (1881-1946)

> His life was gentle and the elements
> So mixed in him that Nature might stand up
> And say to all the world "This was a man".
>
> Julius Caesar

When an inscription was needed for a commemorative plaque I transposed the Shakespearean tribute to Brutus into a more essential precis of those qualities:

THIS WAS A MAN. HIS LIFE WAS GENTLE

He had acute sensitivity, warm generosity and considerable concern for his associates. His sense of fun was lively and lacked any hint of cynicism. His critical faculties were keenly selective. He had innate modesty. Although we were closely associated for more than ten years I had to rely on recent research to reveal some significant facts. In 1930, when he relinquished command of the 4th/5th Territorial Battalion, Cheshire Regiment, he received a letter from General H W Higginson which said:

> "I am writing to thank you for your cordial co-operation and the loyal assistance which you have always given me during the time I have commanded the 55th Division. You have the satisfaction of knowing that you have handed over a very efficient Battalion. You will be very much missed by your old Battalion and the Division."

Also in 1938 after being appointed Honorary Colonel he received a letter from Colonel Arthur Crookenden, saying:

> "I do congratulate you very sincerely on the honour especially as it is one from which Royal prerogative usually bars our officers. They couldn't have a better Honorary Colonel especially as in addition to commanding a Battalion you also had the Brigade."

During the 1939/45 war he was for a period Welfare Officer, Western Command, in Chester. He worked closely with the Red Cross Society in Cheshire.

Understandably he was not able to spend much time during the war with us in Manchester. I think it probable that he had some regret at having to relinquish responsibility but he was not without quiet pride in the progress of the firm he had created.

Personally I have always cherished the memory of our friendship and have been grateful for the opportunity he provided for me to experience some thirty years of stimulating working life: the financial rewards were modest but reasonably adequate.

During discussions with the Trustees and their solicitor and accountant (who was also ours) it was obvious that as Trustees they were reluctant to accept the responsibility for controlling a speculative business such as ours. I agreed but pointed out that the Company had been established and had responsibilities that were unavoidable. I suggested that we should agree temporarily to operate the business as intended, Lilian Watts, the widow, being appointed as a Director. Lilian had been employed by the firm as secretary before her marriage and was therefore familiar with the operations of the company to some extent. This was agreed and we carried on until the end of that financial year, when the accountant suggested that we who were active in the company should make an offer to purchase the business from the Trustees and proposed terms that were advantageous. The Directors and other employees, plus some of the Watts family, agreed to provide the necessary finance for which shares were allotted. A balance of the authorised capital left unsubscribed was available for purchase later. For a time we paid an annual bonus to the staff, some of whom accepted the offer that they could, if they wished, purchase shares with that bonus. Directors of Strand Electric also bought some of the shares. I never succeeded to the title of "the Guvnor". Apart from any derogatory names I might have acquired at times, unknown to me, I seem always to have been referred to as "P.C". I was invariably able to establish a friendly relationship with the staff and with many there was a mutual affection and respect.

Experiments with Nature Cure

In 1944 I was feeling the effects of the long period of exhausting travels and disorganised diets. My digestive mechanism revolted. Acute nausea, dyspepsia and some lassitude demanded attention. My doctor prescribed orthodox "remedies", failing to improve the condition which became gradually worse. When I suggested I might have a few days in bed he agreed with alacrity, having nothing better to propose. He had tentatively suggested that a specialist might help, but not impressed I went to bed and ceased to eat for a time. I then remembered that Karl Birkett had a book written by a man named Harry Benjamin about Nature Cure and fasting. Karl had thought it might be helpful to him in his periodic attacks of hay fever. I borrowed the book and was convinced that a period of fasting could be right for me. After a couple of days the doctor called and was impressed that I seemed to have improved slightly. He admitted the treatment was obviously good for me but said if he recommended it to his patients they would suspect him of being a "quack".

I then read about the existence of Champneys, a former residence of the Rothschilds near Tring, which was a Nature Cure establish-

51

ment. Against my G.P's advice I arranged to visit Champneys for a fortnight. By the time I arrived there my weight had fallen to 8 stones 12 pounds. After I had fasted for five days I had lost the odd 12 pounds and Stanley Leif, the osteopath in charge, decided to end the fast, which had consisted merely of having a tumbler of fruit juice or vegetable extract every four hours between 8.00am and 8.00pm. When the fast ended I had a glass of milk instead of the fruit or vegetable juice, first every four hours but diminishing the intervals each day until it became every hour. By that time I was feeling better and had lost the nausea. In addition to the fasting, each morning I had treatment which would include massage, alternate hot and cold sitz baths, enemas, showers and osteopathy. After the milk period I was given solid food, mostly vegetarian, in a well appointed dining room and I walked round the delightful countryside for a few hours each day. At the end of the fortnight I was vastly improved and returned home well able

One of Rutherford's libellous caricatures in 1945

to follow a normal life and continue the new diet. I became a menace to friends and relatives to whom I prescribed the treatment if they appeared to have the need. I quickly resumed my earlier normal weight of 11 stones 7 pounds which remained constant.

A few years later, after a period of over-work and exposure to cold, I contracted a corneal ulcer on my left eye. For a few months I received treatment prescribed by a specialist who, fortunately, did not order an operation: the trouble partially cleared but constantly returned. I decided to try the Champneys treatment again. Apart from the normal fasting etc the only treatment for the eye was the application each night of a cold compress of shredded raw potato, which I managed to keep in position while asleep. At the end of a fortnight the ulcer cleared up, leaving only a scar on the surface causing a permanent slight deterioration of the sight. Otherwise, the cure was complete. When I saw my specialist and told him how I had been cured he asked if I thought the fasting treatment would be good for his stomach trouble. Without charging a consultant's fee I strongly commended Champneys to him. I don't know whether he took the advice.

On the whole my relatives and friends were very tolerant of my fanaticism about Champneys. In fact several of them did visit the place, including Winnie for her high blood pressure and also Gertrude went for a short stay. On one occasion Humphrey Watts and I had had a refresher course at Champneys for a couple of weeks.

During that time we had some mild amusement and interest due, in part, to the Guvnor's intimate concern for poultry. One of the Champneys patients, a Lancastrian extrovert whose name I forget, had been much involved in the preparation of poultry for sale and he had asserted that he could rough pluck hens for the table at the rate of one per minute. As a result of the consequent protests of disbelief, it was arranged that he should demonstrate his expertise. All the inmates were willing to assemble and to pay a contribution to an agreed charity if the performer could justify his boast. He stipulated that the bird should be delivered to him while still alive and Humphrey Watts, the ex-president of the Poultry Club, arranged to collect a live bird from the Champneys egg producing unit. The Lancastrian donned a borrowed overall and a battered bowler hat as appropriate costume for his performance. There was great amusement and applause when, with a dramatic flourish, the plucked corpse was discarded in less than a minute (49 seconds, I seem to remember). The performer's thumb had, of course, summarily terminated the life of the bird before the plucking began. Chicken was on the menu at dinner the next evening for those who had not become vegetarians!

Regrettably, I allowed my enthusiasm for Nature Cure to lapse. If I hadn't done so I should probably have avoided the slight stroke at the age of 86 which has restricted my mobility since January 1981.

Alterations and additions

During the war it became necessary to review the arrangements with Strand Electric. Much of our joint activity directly involved the Head Office and Works in London. The Branch wages and overheads in Manchester became a Strand Electric responsibility and the profit-sharing arrangement lapsed. My own salary became more realistic. The Branch had its own Sales and Hire Stores and complete staff. It required independent accommodation that could not be adequately housed in the existing buildings. The derelict houses adjoining the Fitups buildings were demolished and a new two-storey structure was erected by Strand Electric, with staircase access between the two buildings at first-floor level. Watts & Corry manufactured a quite impressive separating solid oak door to which the Fire Insurance Inspector objected. He insisted that it be replaced by an approved standard metal door, although the inspector had to admit that our door was much more attractive and probably had better fire resistance. With ill grace we had to accept the dictate of bureaucracy.

On the ground floor was a large store for Hire Stock, an office and work-bench area for repairs. On the first floor were three offices, Sales Store, Demonstration and Lecture Theatre. An open space at the front of the building provided an area for loading and for parking of vehicles.

The Branch had an office staff of book-keepers, estimators, typists, etc. The telephone was shared between the two organisations, the switchboard being in the Watts & Corry building. After a long period as operator, Blanche McGee, who had joined Fitups as a school-leaver, graduated to shorthand typist and later became my secretary. She was a bright lass and was, in fact, the best secretary I ever had. She married Stuart Avison and left when she started a family. When that family (two girls) ceased to need constant maternal attention, Blanche qualified as a school teacher. She still looks too young to be the mother of two adults.

Henry Elder in architectural concentration

There had been considerable internal alterations in the original Fitups buildings during the war. The scenery storage space had been reduced and the limited stocks were transferred to an adjacent disused church and school hall which had been rented. Part of the main building had been altered to accommodate light engineering machines and to provide space for the assembly and testing of units manufactured for the Torpedo Attack Teachers.

A separate department for the planning and equipment of stages had to be created. The building of new schools became a national priority and provision for drama activity was necessary. Many of the architects employed by local authorities needed considerable guidance which had to be supplied by us, mainly Chris Paling, Woody, Cyril Whitter (when he returned) and me. Detailed discussion with architects was usually necessary, followed by written summaries, lay-out drawings and quotations prepared by Paling's department which was ultimately responsible, with Strand Branch, for installations. To avoid the tedious repetition it was decided that a book was necessary. In 1949 I wrote "Stage Planning and Equipment" (115 pages), published by Strand Electric. Henry Elder supplied many of the drawings while he was working in our building in Oldham Road. During the war he had worked as an experimental "boffin" for the Ministry of Aircraft Production and was awarded the OBE. He had assumed RAF uniform for a visit to Japan after the Nagasaki holocaust. We had notions of his joining Watts & Corry staff but in the end he returned to private practice. Later he was offered a professorship at Cornell University in New York State but was refused a visa, much to the surprise of all who knew him. I argued that the decision should be contested and wrote a forceful letter to the offending authority in which I stated that if he were to be prevented from visiting America it would be more the University's loss than Elder's. The sole importance was the refusal of the visa which was unjustified. He did, in fact, receive the permit and in 1960, when I visited him in Ithaca, he informed me that the authorities had received false information about him and that my letter was partly responsible for reversal of the refusal. Henry later was appointed Principal of the Architectural Department of the B C University in Vancouver, where he stayed until retirement. He now lives in Victoria and is much involved with several Canadian academic bodies. He is a man of great ability and integrity.

In the first few years after the war there were many changes in the organisation and operation of Watts & Corry and the Strand Branch. Progressive development was considerably influenced by the enthusiasm and quality of those employees to whom responsibility was necessarily delegated. This is characteristic of small and medium sized firms in the process of development. Large organisations often become too impersonal. Responsible employees can be inhibited in the exercise of their initiative and discretion by the questionable instructions issued by remote managerial theorists, whose lack of knowledge of detail and of the idiosyncrasies of the people concerned. Also, accountancy can too often dictate policy instead of it being merely a useful servant of management.

Scenery for Television

One of the most important factors in the development of Watts &

Corry was the creation of television studios in Manchester. In 1955 the BBC began to broadcast TV programmes from temporary premises in Rusholme without any workshop for building the settings they required. They were therefore very pleased to have the facilities we were able to offer. Their resident designer, Kenneth Lawson, discussed with us the settings required, which we supplied on hire. Their early needs were modest and could be mainly met with our existing facilities. Later, when Granada and ABC shared the Independent TV broadcasts from Manchester, they considerably increased demand for our services. ABC studios were created in their Didsbury Capitol Cinema but they were not allowed to build workshops in what is a suburban residential area and their depen-

Scenery for television being constructed in Watts & Corry studio

ence on Watts & Corry was vital. Granada built entirely new and extensive premises near to the Opera House in the centre of the city, including well-equipped workshops. In the early days before the Granada building was complete, the two TV companies shared the Capitol Studios and both had to rely on us to provide the settings. Even when Granada's new building was finished they still had to depend on us to supplement their scenic production. It quickly became obvious that we had to increase our facilities. We had engaged additional staff and purchased a vacated bakery in Failsworth. It was a two-storey building. Although the ceilings were not as high as desirable we created a commodious joiners' workshop at first floor level, the ground floor being available for assembly, painting and storage: a large open area at the rear provided excellent space for loading vans and the parking of employees' cars. All the joiners were transferred to the bakery together with the increased staff of scenic artists, interior decorators, other craftsmen and the clerical workers. Stuart Avison managed the department, with Frank McCormick in charge of the workshop, and Phil Cartlitch supervised the completion, painting and handling of the scenery. It was, in effect, a comprehensive separate unit operating very profitably until the work was drastically restricted by TV personnel taking what would be nowadays euphemistically referred to as "industrial action" - meaning "inaction", of course. This strike played havoc with our profit and loss accounts for a period, the painful emphasis being on loss. For a period I refrained from drawing a salary from Watts & Corry and in due course increased my holding of shares to the extent of the money owed to me. In the long run this proved to be advantageous!

Domestic Changes

In 1944 I sold the house in Garner's Lane and bought a larger, Victorian double-fronted house named Woodstock on Bramhall Lane, which my wife had often visited in earlier days. Owing to pressure from the people who had bought the Garner's Lane house we moved earlier than we wished, which proved to be fortunate for us. While we were struggling to settle in the new house, just prior to Christmas, a German flying bomb (popularly known at the time as a "doodle bug") fell within a few hundred yards of the house we had left and caused quite considerable damage. As the bomb fell into a sand pit the main damage was caused by blast, which we were pleased to have escaped.

We lived happily at Woodstock for fifteen years which ended tragically. In 1960 my wife suffered a stroke and for several months we had a nurse living on the premises. At the age of 66 my wife died. Patrick and I decided against employing a housekeeper, who would have been a necessity had we remained at Woodstock. We arranged to rent a new flat, included in an ambitious development in Didsbury. This was not completed as early as promised and for a period of about six months we lived at the Edge Hotel on Alderley Edge, which enabled us to become adjusted to loss of the spaciousness of Woodstock and to accept the restricted accommodation of a flat. Although we managed reasonably well, with the aid of a daily help, we agreed that flat life was not our choice for a permanent arrangement. Early in 1963 we purchased a three-bedroomed detached house with attractive gardens. We organised many alterations and additions and took up residence at 4 Harefield Drive in December 1963, where we have lived up to the present.

As is recorded later, Patrick resigned from the Watts & Corry organisation in 1968, after the take-over by Rank, and did not seek other employment. A London firm of importers bought the house next door to accommodate their representatives and overseas people when visiting customers in the area. It was arranged with Patrick that he would supervise the premises, arrange for supplies of food and drink and also attend to the garden, a spare time job which proved to be useful.

When we lost our daily help Patrick took on the responsibility of our housework, which he has performed even better than the hired help.

Family group of the Burns, Birketts and Corrys about 1959

PART FIVE
Varied Projects after 1946

Early in the post-war period Watts & Corry and the Strand Branch obtained contracts for the staging of a number of celebratory productions. The City of Lichfield celebrated the 750th Anniversary of the Cathedral. Frank Napier was engaged to present a modern miracle play, "The Just Vengeance", written specially by Dorothy M Sayers. We erected a three-tiered stage which filled the nave and provided a comprehensive selection of spots and floods controlled by portable interlocking boards to create flexible lighting. The installation was supervised by Woody. It was a popular and impressive show.

A pageant to celebrate the 150th Anniversary of Newton Chambers Ltd, a mammoth firm of steel manufacturers, was staged in the City Hall, Sheffield. It was written by Dr L du Garde Peach and produced by Heath Joyce. The scenery had not only a decorative or realistic purpose, it had to conceal the organ console and other intrusive features. There was a comprehensive lighting fit-up which coped with over 400 lighting cues. Princess Margaret attended the opening. The audience, bidden to stand for her entrance, were evidently intimidated to silence: the entrance, therefore, had a solemnity that was not exactly appropriate to a festival occasion.

Shortly afterwards Nottingham celebrated 500 years of something or other by a spectacular show in the Ice Stadium (without ice), again having the Heath Joyce and Laurie Peach combination. Within a week the Stadium was transformed into a "theatre" with a large stage and an impressive lighting fit-up of 190 lanterns. It was unusual for us to work in such an environment without ice.

We had considerable experience of working with cold feet at the Ice Drome on the Pleasure Beach at Blackpool, of which a Mr Thompson was the dynamic controller. He had an enthusiastic concern for the Ice Drome, in which he presented a colourful production each summer. Invariably we were involved with the lighting effects. The entire lighting installation was by Strand Electric and during the years we kept the equipment up to date. When we installed remote control we required a building at the rear for the dimmer bank. Thompson was a man who was unable to tolerate delays, and although at that time building licences were necessary, he gave instructions for the construction to be started. The concrete floor had been laid when the building inspector notified his intention to examine the site before a licence could be issued. Thompson at once gave instruction for a load of coke to be tipped on the concrete area before the inspector arrived and had to assume that the coke was intended for the central heating boiler. The licence was obtained, the coke cleared away and building proceeded. I usually attended the dress rehearsals of the summer show and on one occasion he was grimly amused when I refused a demand by the lady producer (Bettina Merson by name) for more red light to give the needed fire effect. I had to point out that fire was more deep amber than the red she wanted.

Talking of fire reminds me that on July 12th 1949 I read in my newspaper, when breakfasting at the Bull and Royal Hotel, Preston, that there had been a serious conflagration after the previous night's show in the Ice Drome and so I decided to drive to Blackpool. When I arrived an irate Thompson grumbled that he hadn't been able to get in touch with me earlier. It was about 10.00am. The steel girders supporting the roof had been badly twisted and all our suspended lanterns (about 150) had crashed to the ice. Many needed considerable repair: others had to be replaced. Thompson said he intended to re-open on 17th August ... and, of course, he did. He usually got what he wanted. His peremptory bark was much worse than his bite and I liked the man. We did a lot of work for him in other parts of the Pleasure Beach.

Earlier in 1949 I had received an "invitation" to visit him at his home on a Sunday, not merely to have lunch with him but to discuss a project for Morecambe, where he intended to put on another ice show. He had purchased a Bellman hangar and had it transformed into a theatre seating 1,800. There was an ice stage, 50 feet x 50 feet, for which we had to supply and install the lighting equipment, which included over 100 lanterns, 4 Sunspot arcs and a dimmer bank. As was usual, everybody concerned had to work at the double to meet his opening date.

At Blackpool, Thompson invariably attended dress rehearsals and his voice was usually strong enough to halt the company when necessary. On one occasion he found he could not compete successfully against the orchestra and at the next rehearsal he produced a revolver whose blank shots were more efficient! After that, many of us referred to him as Trigger Thompson with affectionate amusement.

Another occasion when a theatre fire was good for our business was when the Theatre Royal, Hanley, was partially destroyed. It was restored and re-equipped in the summer of 1951. Before the fire I had refused to quote for a type of automatic colour control which was having a short popularity. Although we could offer a similar control (intended for ballrooms, etc, but not suitable for the stage) I suggested a type that was suitable. My advice was not accepted and the unsuitable control was actually purchased. After the fire I was called to Hanley again. The previous episode was ignored completely and I received orders for all the stage equipment, which included the entire lighting installation, safety curtain, counter-weighted suspension gear, proscenium curtain, all draperies and stage accessories. It is gratifying when experience can convince erring customers that they are not always right.

My next incendiary experience was with Hell Fire!. In 1951 the York Cycle of Mystery Plays was revived in a modern version. They were originally performed in the 14th century by the York Craft Guilds each year on Corpus Christi Day. Originally there were 48 plays, each performed on a vehicle known as a "pageant", which was pushed through the streets, following in sequence to arranged sites in the city. This new version had been adapted to modern speech and dialect by Doctor Purvis of York Minster. The performance was staged in the ruins of St Mary's Abbey. A platform behind the Gothic arches provided a significant eminence for paradise from which God the Father opened the show with impressive sonority. In one corner a large raised platform served variously as the Garden of Eden, Gethsemane, Calvary and, at ground level, provided the Tomb. A long staircase led to the heavenly platform. A traditionally grotesque Hell's Mouth dominated the corner on stage left. Small individual stages suggested the 14th century "pageants" and served as the "houses" of Caiaphas, Pontius Pilate etc, and as the Nativity Stable. A tubular steel structure created the large auditorium and enabled us to have a number of tall towers for the stage floods and spots. A 40 feet high control room at the rear of the stand housed a formidable collection of portable dimmer boards and the sound amplification equipment, all under the control of Herbert Hughes, who cued the operators. Changes of scene were localised by cross fading during a performance with only one interval. There was a liberal variety and quantity of lanterns and not a few impressive effects, one of which gave me great joy. One of the professional actors (named Westbrook), a man of impressive physique, played the part of the archangel on whom Jesus called during his violent confrontation with the Devil in lurid lighting in the Hell's Mouth area. For this entrance the actor volunteered to mount in the darkness a tall portion of the ruins. Fading-in an intense soft edged spot (used solely for this purpose) it was possible for the archangel, clad in "golden" armour to appear with a sword upraised, apparently in space. Its impressive effect was recently confirmed for me, when my niece, who had seen the show about thirty years previously, said what she particularly remembered of it was the appearance of the archangel in the darkness.

The show was directed by Martin Browne, who let me have freedom with the lighting. I had invaluable assistance from Herbert Hughes, who also supervised the installation and operation during rehearsal and performance. We could not begin lighting rehearsals until after sunset and the cast had been dismissed, usually about 11.00pm. On one occasion we finished setting the lighting as the June dawn broke with the delightful musical approval of the waking birds.

There was a very large cast, mostly amateur with about a dozen professionals. The crowd scenes were balletically controlled by Geraldine Stephenson with expert artistry. The performances lasted for three weeks and were subsequently repeated at three yearly intervals with changes of casts and direction: not always for the better. I was involved in four of them. An arduous but very exciting and rewarding task.

At Colwyn Bay in 1947 we began a long annual association with the Welsh National Eisteddfod. Each year the site alternates between North and South Wales, with much local competition for organising this festival of the arts with special emphasis on the musical events. A large sectional building with a seating capacity of several thousand is erected. The Eisteddfod itself lasts for one week only (the first in August), after which the building is dismantled and transferred to the site chosen for the following year. It was our job to install (and dismantle) the lighting equipment and all the stage furnishing. The latter was comparatively simple but the lighting was, of course, considerably complicated. It was always supervised by Harry Greaves, who acquired a proprietary interest in the Eisteddfod (and a Welsh wife) in the process. He was a conscientiously reliable and competent technician who was universally popular in spite of a misleading pessimistic tendency which was more of a superficial attitude than a basic characteristic.

When the Welsh instituted an annual international Eisteddfod at Llangollen it was almost inevitable that we should undertake the less arduous task of fitting up the equipment needed each July in a large marquee always on the same site. Harry's obligations to the "National" land of his father-in-law prevented him from taking responsibilities to the Internationalist Authorities.

Son et Lumiere

For a rather short period there was some interest in this type of production imported from France, where it was a tourist attraction. The basic need was for a building of architectural quality with a history of dramatic significance which could be emphasised by colour lighting and appropriate sound. I had not seen any of the French presentations but did see and disapprove of the efforts in this country and one in Athens, which I regarded as a disastrous failure to use effectively the majesty of the Acropolis. In each of the programmes I have seen, it was the regrettable practice to use recorded voices to represent the people who were supposed to be involved in some historical episode within the building (or often even outside its precincts), the accompanying lighting effects having no relevance whatever. In 1958 I was asked to discuss with Lord Hertford the possibility of arranging a Son et Lumiere presentation at his home, Ragley Hall in Worcestershire. Although I realised that the building lacked architectural quality and was limited in historical drama, I was tempted to test my convictions and agreed to undertake the job if I could write the script and direct the whole show. The only disembodied voice I used was that of Michael Redgrave, whose speeches linked together the various episodes, with recorded music and sound effects and with appropriate comment. In devising the lighting and choosing the music I again had the assistance of Herbert Hughes, who also supervised the installation and operation of the lighting. Although the Hall lacks architectural significance, it adequately reflected colour and some visual suggestions. Much use was made of a variety of internal lighting of rooms appropriate to the comment and of exterior effects such as the movement of the illumination of trees as a body of chanting monks were assumed to be passing through the forest.

It was a stimulating exercise and proved, to me at any rate, that my theories had been correct.

Theatre Planning

For many years a lot of us wrote profusely, lectured extensively and attended conferences in many parts of the world, discussing the types of community theatres that should be provided (usually at public expense) for both professional and amateur performances. These discussions also frequently included provision for dramatic education in schools, colleges, universities, leisure centres and similar projects. There was an interesting lack of uniformity of ideas and convictions and not a little of expensive experiment.

There was a proliferation of self appointed "experts" and in 1960 Stephen Joseph organised the creation of the Society of Theatre Consultants of which my colleague, Fred Bentham, and I were founder members. This Society is able to offer consultants of differing ideas and experience for choice by organisations concerned with creation or alteration of theatres. Society members have been consultants for most theatres built in recent years, including the National Theatre and The Barbican in London. Local authorities appointed their own Drama Advisers, ensuring interesting scope for clash of extravagant ideas.

It would be impossible (and not particularly important) to attempt even to list the hundreds of projects with which we were involved during the years, but a typical variety of a selected few could, perhaps, be of interest.

MIDDLESBROUGH LITTLE THEATRE

An enterprising amateur company under the energetic leadership of David Sillars had for many years accumulated funds to enable them to build a theatre. They achieved this ambition in 1958 at a cost of £50,000 free of debt when opened: it was an impressive amount in those days. The architects were Henry Elder and his volatile partner Enrico de Pierro. It is a proscenium type theatre without a fly-tower but having a generous stage area (70ft width, 40ft depth) and has a seating capacity of 500. The theatre is used by several amateur dramatic and operatic societies and by touring professionals. As the Society's President, Tyrone Guthrie, was in America, John Gielgud agreed to officiate at the opening ceremony.

ROSEHILL THEATRE, CUMBRIA

This is an exquisite small theatre built in 1959 for the Rosehill Arts Society in the grounds of the home of one Miki Sekers (later "Sir Nicholas", no less) an ebullient refugee from Budapest who had established a prosperous silk fabric manufacturing business in Whitehaven. Not surprisingly, the interior of the theatre was liberally decorated with silken materials (rose colour of course) to Oliver Messel's adaptation of Georgian design. I was rash enough to appear on the site a week before the opening to find the place in a state of disorderly chaos and with greater rashness I impressed on Miki the obvious need of an individual in charge to direct proceedings. Shortly afterwards everybody was assembled to be informed that I was from then in charge and had to be obeyed. I should have had sense enough to keep my big mouth shut! But it was quite interesting. During my supervisory prowling I discovered that sight-lines from the balcony were deplorable. I protested to Miki and the next morning a gang of men from the silk mill were busy reorganising the floor and raising the seats. The day before the opening I had to organise and take charge of rehearsals for Emlyn Williams, who was giving his solo performance, and for Dame Peggy Ashcroft, who had to deliver an impressive poetic prologue to "Ring Up The Curtain". The latter sought my comment and I was more than flattered to be a temporary director of the charming professional. Emlyn Williams knew exactly what he wanted and I had merely to see that he got it. He also had his own stage manager on the job. For his performance I occupied the prompt corner and was vastly impressed by his perfect technique observed at close quarters.

RICHMOND THEATRE

This is the Yorkshire town of which the Lass of Richmond Hill is alleged to have been a resident. The theatre dates back to 1788 and is one of the few Georgian theatres that had remained reasonably intact and was, therefore, a delight to Richard Southern, who was an ardent researcher and had been engaged to investigate the history of the building. It was one of a circuit in Yorkshire; others being in Harrogate, Ripon, Northallerton and Beverley, owned by a Samuel Butler. Members of his companies had been Edmund Kean, Kemble, Macready, Mrs Siddons, Jane Wallis and others who became stars of the period. After 1841 the theatre had served as a corn chandler's warehouse, furniture store and a salvage depot, fortunately leaving the basic features reasonably intact. In 1949 a York architect, with Southern as consultant, prepared restoration plans and an attempt to raise £15,000 was made. It had little success until in 1960 the Georgian Theatre (Richmond) Trust was formed and under the vital leadership of Lady Crathorne made significant progress. Restoration was completed in 1962.

The auditorium is small, measuring 26ft by 24ft, which is practically the size of the stage. A set of Georgian scenery was discovered and was renovated by Watts & Corry's artists. Period-type forms were installed with slightly extended gaps to allow for the greater seating space essential for modern audiences. Candles could not provide the lighting, which was as discreet as possible. The proscenium curtain, a reefer type, was made from a specially dyed fabric representing as nearly as possible the green baize of the period. The theatre is primarily a tourist museum attraction but is occasionally used for performances.

The opening of the restored theatre was an important civic affair and was attended by Dames Sybil Thorndike and Edith Evans: Ivor Brown contributed rhymed verse in which each of us involved in the project was mentioned in appropriate tribute.

HOLME-ON-SPALDING MOOR VILLAGE THEATRE

This was a project organised by another adventurous body of amateurs. After many years operating in a wooden structure that had originally served as a multi-purpose hall, in the 1914-18 war the Holme Players decided to buy the site and hoped to build a new theatre. In 1954 a York architect was asked to prepare plans but when the cost was estimated at £15,000 (their limit was £9,000) Miles Hutchinson, the village doctor, explored the possibility of building the new hall with local labour. He discovered a number of skilled building workers and a lot of unskilled volunteers, all of whom agreed to work unpaid in their leisure time. The doctor insisted that each volunteer should be credited with the hourly rate for the job, the amounts thus earned being treated as contributions to the fund. 16,000 hours of this voluntary labour were recorded, the highest individual total being 1,900 hours credited to a cabinetmaker working as a joiner. I was delighted to be their voluntary stage consultant.

VICTORIA THEATRE, STOKE-ON-TRENT

For many years Stephen Joseph (son of Hermione Gingold) had

toured a professional company presenting theatre-in-the-round, a type which he favoured. During quite a considerable period he had a permanent company performing at Newcastle-under-Lyme (and other towns) in the winter and in Scarborough each summer. He achieved popularity in both towns and was eager to establish his own theatre. The Victoria Cinema quite near to Newcastle became available. With our co-operation he transformed it into a theatre with a centre stage, 24ft by 20ft, with 345 seats evenly distributed round that acting area, and opened it in 1962. At that time it was the only professional theatre-in-the-round. It is still operating successfully. When Stephen became a lecturer at the Manchester University he appointed Peter Cheeseman to direct the theatre for him. In 1967 at the age of only 46 after a distressing illness Stephen died at his home in Scarborough. The theatre could ill afford to lose him. He was a man of great intelligence and integrity and had strong convictions, about which he could be fluently articulate. He could be vigorously combative in public argument but had a basic sensitivity that was endearing. During the war he served with the Navy and was awarded a DSO. It is fitting that a theatre-in-the-round bearing his name has been established in Scarborough.

Watts & Corry Ltd merge with Strand Electric

In 1964 we considered the possibility of offering to the existing shareholders the opportunity of purchasing the unsubscribed balance of the shares. This prompted Sheridan to suggest that Strand Electric should take over the company. At that time I was 70 years old and realised that retirement, more or less imminent, could cause some concern about future control. The combination of the two firms was quite a logical possibility and Strand accepted our accountants' valuation. The deal was completed with some capital gain to the shareholders.

It was also in 1964 that Strand Electric celebrated its Golden Jubilee by a special historical issue of TABS and an impressive jamboree at the Dorchester Hotel attended by 750 guests. We were by that time part of the Strand Group, which thought it desirable to extend its manufacturing facilities. Our Ken Mould had created a light engineering department with Frank Watson in charge of the electrical section. It would have been impossible to provide accommodation for the suggested manufacture in the Oldham Road premises and we found a disused textile mill in Gorton which Strand decided to purchase. After alterations it was possible to provide more than adequate accommodation for all activities, apart from the TV Scenery Section now well established in the former bakery. The Gorton factory occupied an extensive site on which a large car park was provided, still leaving room for additions to the buildings, if required. Ken Mould created the department to cope with the lighting equipment manufacture and supervised the whole factory as Works Manager. The Strand Hire and Sales Stores, a Demonstration Theatre and several offices were accommodated in a building adjoining the main factory. The limited stock of stage scenery was disposed of and Ernest Lee transferred to the Stage Equipment Section managed by Joseph Clarke. The Oldham Road buildings were sold and removal was completed during the summer of 1965.

International Travel

Between 1954 and 1960 Fred Bentham and I visited many parts of the USA and Canada, as well as several European cities, attending conferences, inspecting theatres and sometimes lecturing. In 1963 I decided to visit Minneapolis to attend an exhibition and to see performances at the newly opened Tyrone Guthrie Theatre. From there I went to stay a few days with Henry Elder in Vancouver. From Vancouver I went on to San Francisco, then crossed the Pacific to Sydney, spending one night en route in Honolulu. In Australia I visited Brisbane, Canberra, Melbourne, Adelaide and stayed a week with relatives in Perth: then across the Indian Ocean to Johannesburg via Mauritius, another one night stay. In Africa I lectured in Johannesburg, Pretoria, Cape Town, Durban, Bloemfontein, and also relaxed for a couple of days in the Kruger Game Reserve but failed to rise early enough to see the lions! I lectured mainly on stage lighting and met many interesting people. I was, however, rather conscious of apartheid and on one occasion (in Pretoria, I think) I was slightly put out by being introduced to the audience in Afrikaans, on which I commented rather sardonically, I fear.

I left South Africa for Cairo en route to Athens and after a couple of days there inspecting some relics of the earliest theatres and witnessing a not very distinguished performance of Son et Lumiere,

Karl, Gertrude and Deirdre Birkett with author on the "Queen Mary" in 1961

which failed to make something significant of the opportunities presented by the incomparable setting of the Parthenon, I returned to London. I had achieved 63 days of interesting journeyings of more than 36,000 miles on 23 flights. Consistently I flew East to West, which I have always found to be less fatiguing than flying long journeys West to East: something to do with the time factor, I think.

Drama School in Ireland

In 1966 I was invited by the Irish Drama League to be one of the tutors at a week's Drama School open to members of affiliated societies. There was a remarkably large and enthusiastic attendance of friendly students. We all had living accommodation at the Gormanston College during their holiday period in July.

In the protracted daily and late nightly sessions there was lively participation. Mornings and evenings were devoted to lectures and

The author pretending to be a Franciscan Friar at Gormaston College, a tutor at the Irish Drama League Summer School, 1966

discussions; each afternoon sundry groups were rehearsing scenes from various plays to be performed on the Friday evening; the tutors toured the groups to offer advice and criticism. One of the rehearsals I "inspected" was an act of "School for Scandal". Joseph Surface was being played by one of the R.C fathers, a member of the Gormanston staff. Rather incongruously, the actor rehearsed in his monk's habit. I suggested he should don less formal garb for the rehearsals but asked him to bring his habit, which I should like to wear for a memento photograph. The next day he rehearsed in sporting attire and I donned the priestly habit. I was complimented by a fellow tutor on having acquired a good habit, for a change! One of the students claimed that I looked more authentic than any normal wearer of the "costume", which I found very comfortable and attractive.

The ending of the Gormanston drama week coincided with the opening of the newly built Abbey Theatre on Saturday, 18th July 1966. The opening ceremony was performed by President de Valera, an indication that the new Abbey should be regarded as the Irish national theatre. The original theatre had been destroyed by fire on 18th July 1951. I was a member of a party which included Lorean and Kevin Bourke of the Strand Electric Dublin Branch and their brother in law, Eamonn Andrews. It was a very convivial evening. I was much impressed by the theatre: rather less so by a stage performance which betrayed signs of hurried preparation.

House in Synge Street, Dublin, stated to be the birthplace of "Bernard Shaw, author of many plays" - an amusing understatement.

PART SIX
Actor, Director and Writer

From the record of my early years it would not be clear why Humphrey Watts invited me to take charge of Fitups in 1936. A summary of my independent theatre experience should serve to explain. As the beginning of my theatrical life is a logical place at which to start, I shall first deal with my experience in the presentation of plays on the stage as actor and director (or producer, which term was in my time universally employed in the theatre). Later, under the influence of Radio and Television custom, the theatre adopted "director" for the person who controlled the actual detail of performance in rehearsal. I am inclined to use either term for the same function.

Actor and Producer

My first appearances on stage at the age of about 16 were in performances by the Stockport Clarion Players produced by one R J Smith. I don't remember what minor parts I first played but an early one was my first Shaw character, a Cockney conscript soldier, in his one-act play "Press Cuttings". I also played one or two parts for the Marple Dramatic Society in plays also produced by R J Smith.

I first appeared in a Garrick Society production in 1912 when Galsworthy's "Strife" was produced at the Stockport Theatre Royal. I was merely an anonymous member of the crowd scene, but in 1915 I played Peter Simple in "The Merry Wives of Windsor", my first part for the Garrick. I was not a member when invited (the war had narrowed their choice of male members) and during the run of the show I joined the Society. In 1916 I played the lead in "The Probationer" by Anthony Rowley, my first performance in the Society's own rooms at Cobden Place in Wellington Street. There was a diminutive stage and audience of about a hundred. Each play was presented as a "private performance" for a week, always to a full house. Tickets of invitation were free, there being a "silver collection" which ensured a minimum contribution of three pence, the smallest silver coin! After my return from the Army in 1919 I played in three productions each season until 1923 when I produced "Paolo and Francesca" by Stephen Phillips, my first for the Society. It was also one of the earliest shows in what was known as the Garrick Hall. The Society had formed a limited company in 1920 to acquire a disused warehouse in Wellington Road which it transformed into a theatre. There have since been many alterations and additions to those premises and the limited company has been replaced by a Trust. In 1927 I played Jack Tanner in "Man and Superman", the first of the major Shavian roles; in 1934 and again in 1950, I played King Magnus in "The Apple Cart": in 1935 I played Drinkwater in "Captain Brassbound's Conversion". Some years later I produced "Don Juan in Hell" and played the Don. In "Man of Destiny" I played Napoleon. In "Heartbreak House" I played Shotover. I was engaged by various organisations to produce plays for them, including the Wilmslow Green Room Society, for whom I produced at least one play each year (a total of 18) between 1927 and 1936, which included several Shaw plays, ("The Devil's Disciple", "Pygmalion", "Caesar and Cleopatra") and others by less exalted playwrights. Altogether I produced for more than a dozen societies. For the Bolton Little Theatre I produced eight shows, mainly Shaw and Shakespeare, the latter including "King Lear". Although Shaw was the favourite in my repertoire, the productions were, in fact, very varied and included Noel Coward, Galsworthy, Edgar Wallace, Moliere, A A Milne and many of the less well-known dramatists.

Altogether, as nearly as I can recall, I produced a total of more than 65 plays and acted over 50 parts. The latter rarely, if ever, were juvenile leads. I suppose I had a rather sardonic appearance until my hair turned grey, then white, adding a little distinction! I was usually cast for what are wrongly described as "character parts". All theatrical parts are (or should be) "characters". The so called character parts are usually the more interesting to perform.

When I became an experienced producer I was in complete command until the final dress rehearsal, after which I handed over responsibility to the stage manager and rarely watched a subsequent performance. As an obligation I attended the opening night's performance but later I couldn't bear to witness how far it fell short of the ideal for which I had striven. On occasion, if I had introduced some novel effect I would watch that during several performances just to test the audience reactions. On the whole I enjoyed acting more than directing, but both could be satisfying and sometimes disappointing.

In 1933 I was engaged to devise and produce a Revue for the Wilmslow Green Room Society and wrote a series of five burlesque sketches entitled "Cupid's Cavalcade", contrasting the techniques of mating by male and female from the pre-historic to the future. The scenes, each lasting about ten minutes, were linked by the recital of rhyming couplets by the compere.

Pre-historic: This was a burlesqued mime, the only spoken expressions being Oh! and Ah!

Early Romantic: A baritone sang "The Lute Player" to which three actors mimed dramatically behind a gauze.

Victorian: An exaggerated burlesque of a matrimonial proposal of the period. Three actors.

Modern: Bright young things of the thirties, slightly imitating the style of Noel Coward. Two actors.

Future: Unmarried Male and Female. Called up for service in the Matrimonial Corps of a Corporate State. Marriage ceremony conducted by a Sergeant Registrar. Three actors.

The Wilmslow people were rather apprehensive and pressed me to make alterations. I refused emphatically and after some argument I withdrew it.

About a year later the Stockport Garrick Society were conferring honorary membership on William Armstrong, the director of the Liverpool Repertory Theatre. They wanted to put on a show for the evening of the ceremony and asked me to provide something. I offered to stage "Cupid's Cavalcade" and without reading it they agreed. It was quite a success and after the show Armstrong asked me to write the last episode into a one-act play and let him have it for a possible production in Liverpool. I added two characters, a bumptious female Controller of the Creche and an Orderly who was classified as Socially Defective, making a total of five, three men and two women. The playing time was about half an hour: I gave it the title of "Cupid Rampant". After some delay Armstrong returned the play. His reader was critical, particularly of the dictated marriage business. It was also thought it would not be popular with his audience which apparently included sympathisers with the Corporate State idea and about that time criticism of the Nazis, of whom the play was critical by implication, was not universally favoured. For that reason, Armstrong thought a licence could be refused. This provoked me into testing the Lord Chamberlain. I enlisted a cast and decided to play the part of the Orderly myself. We called ourselves the Stockport Stage Society and I entered the play for the Blackpool Drama Festival in 1935. We played to a packed audience at the Opera House, Blackpool. It was received well. According to the press the next morning "Cupid Rampant swept the audience by storm" and the adjudicator, Sladen Smith, said: "It is probably too witty and intelligent for most revues".

Author receiving prize for best original play (Cupid Rampant) at Blackpool Festival

For the best original play I received a cheque and, for a period of a year, a silver cup which had originally served as a prize in a sailing competition. Its design was rather extravagantly nautical. The man who donated it, a Blackpool jeweller, wearing a velvet jacket with miniature watches for buttons, assured me it was "t'best cup in t'show": after the year I relinquished it without tears. The performance won the prize for the best comedy and the actor who played the Sergeant Registrar received a prize for the best individual performance.

The play was published in a book containing eight one-act plays that had won first prizes in Drama Festivals. Samuel French Ltd agreed to act as agents and printed separate copies. It was produced in many parts of this country and in various parts of the Commonwealth. I received quite useful sums in royalties: one guinea per performance. I had some malicious satisfaction in having proved Armstrong to be wrong!

In 1935 my wife, Winifred, was organising a Garrick social and asked me to provide a stage performance for the event. I had read a short story in a newspaper which I thought could be made into a play. With the consent of the writer I made considerable alterations of the plot and produced a one-act play with the title "Check". It played quite well and I later entered it at Drama Festivals in Buxton and Morecambe. It won the original play prize at the latter.

At times I have thought seriously of making attempts at playwriting but basically I think I am more of a critical commentator than a creative writer. I did make one abortive attempt. In writing for a very tentative plot one of the characters intended to be the lead got quite out of hand and made the plot impossible. I gave up in disgust.

Writing

My contributions to TABS, the quarterly journal published by Strand Electric, covered a wide variety of theatrical subjects over the years. TABS first appeared in 1937 in simple form. With the outbreak of war publication ceased. After the issue in April 1939 there were more important matters compelling our attention but publication was resumed in September 1946 in rather more impressive format.

The journal was issued free to all who took the trouble to get their names on the mailing list. The circulation ultimately exceeded 20,000 per issue; it was distributed all over the world.

I contributed to every one of the first twenty-five numbers and when I last estimated the number of articles I had written, a few years ago, the total exceeded 200,000 words in more than 120 issues. In December 1946 I began what became known as "The Must Series", giving acidulated comment and instruction to all and sundry concerned with play production, such as "Stage Managers Must Manage", "Producers Must Produce", "Lighting Artists Must Light", "Critics Must Criticise", "Playwrights Must Write Plays", "Actors Must Act", "Props Must Find Props" and so on. The series concluded in 1951 with "Everybody Must Do Everything". The comments were very light-hearted and appeared to be popular. Thereafter I dealt with a wide variety of subjects. I was rather pleased by my criticism of the Drury Lane performance of "My Fair Lady" under the title "Fabulous Lady".

Books and Booklets

In 1938 Strand Electric had issued a booklet I had written about stage lighting in schools, etc. It quoted a report issued by the Board of Education of which the following is a significant extract:

"It is worth adding a note on the value of dramatic performances as an aid to appreciation. The drama has now a sure footing in all schools and its usefulness in cultivating self-confidence and good speech and developing initiative need not be stressed".

In 1949 I wrote "Stage Planning and "Equipment" which was published by Strand Electric. This I wrote partly in self-defence. At the time new schools were being planned and I was calling on numerous architects responsible for such buildings. Invariably I found it necessary to go into considerable detail and usually it was essential to follow up the call with written amplification of what had been discussed. The book examined the problems exhaustively. There was then no comparable book published and Strand Electric decided to produce it. Five thousand copies were printed at a selling price of five shillings each (which was the approximate cost price) but free copies were sent to the Chief Architects of most of the local authorities. After the supplies were exhausted, in 1953 I compressed its 116 pages into a 26 page booklet. Of this booklet 60,000 copies were ultimately printed (six editions) and circulated throughout the English-speaking countries. It was then revised completely to consider the developments of stage techniques and of later planning problems.

In 1953 "Lighting the Stage", which had been commissioned by Pitman, was published. It had a foreword written by Tyrone Guthrie for whose comment I was grateful. The following has been extracted from his Foreword:

"Now what I like and admire about Mr Corry is that he has the qualifications of an expert - wide technical knowledge, a life-long experience of and an enthusiastic love for the theatre. But he never uses these qualifications to present himself as a know-all. He never pontificates. He never says: 'This is the Right Way; do what I tell you and you can't go wrong.'

Mr Corry offers the fruit of his knowledge and experience in what I find a most easy and apprehensible manner, with the very minimum of jargon and with none of that pretentious suggestion, so usual in theatrical writing, that the topic is of universal and epoch-making importance. He writes simply, humbly and with a sense of proportion. From his experience he proceeds to offer not merely technical assistance but general advice. And he relates the particular branch of theatrical craftmanship with which he is principally concerned to the whole concept of play-production. If he draws general conclusions, they are always moderately and modestly expressed, and do not preclude the possibility of exceptions; if he offers advice, it is always sensible and never dogmatic.

I do not always agree with Mr Corry. On quite a number of points my views and his diverge. But even where most inclined to argue, I found myself disarmed by the author's good-tempered assumption that one was at liberty to argue; that there is in fact, no single Right Way".

In my own Preface I had stated:

"In dealing with stage lighting as an art, not as a science, it is inevitable that facts and opinions should be stated with a bias of personal preference likely to provoke some controversy. This is all to the good. When the theatre ceases to be controversial it will be dead".

The book was reasonably successful and had two or more editions.

In 1959 Pitman added "Planning the Stage" and the jacket proclaimed "Percy Corry, Author of 'Lighting the Stage'." I had completed the draft which was in my briefcase at home, preparatory to a visit to Pitman's in London the next day. The house was burgled during the night and the case was one of the few articles of any significance that was stolen. I had, therefore, to re-write the whole book as I hadn't a copy. Years afterwards the police recovered the briefcase but the thief, unimpressed by my words of wisdom, had destroyed the script.

In the meantime the Museum Press, a subsidiary of Pitman's, had commissioned me to write "Amateur Theatrecraft", published in 1960. Judging by the royalties I received it was reasonably successful.

Corry in characteristic concentration - 1964

In 1954 I wrote a booklet of 16 pages, "Stage Lighting on a Shoestring", which was provoked by the reactions of an audience of schoolmasters in Sheffield after I had lectured. They complained that our publications over-estimated the amounts they were likely to be able to spend on equipment. They referred to a scheme we estimated to cost about £300 but said they were lucky if they could get £30 to spend. On my way home I reflected that there must be many in this position and on the next day I wrote the booklet, "Stage Lighting on a Shoestring", advising them what could be done at little expense to improve their lighting with the possibility of gradually adding to their equipment in the future. Strand Electric at once published the booklet which had a considerable circulation in the Commonwealth.

In 1974 Pitman's published my book "Community Theatres", which was an enlargement of the Theatre Planning problems, taking into account the considerable developments and having in view possible local and national subsidies. I had the collaboration of Robert Adams, a Sheffield architect with whom I had worked on many projects. It was rather less popular than I had hoped and royalties received were but modest. Many other books on theatre subjects had been published and by that time Pitman's had, I think, lost interest and concern for their Theatre and Stage series.

Until after my retirement in 1965 my contributions to TABS and other publications by Strand Electric were not paid for. Pecuniary reward was never the important consideration. It was, however, quite pleasurable to receive periodical cheques for the royalties earned by the books and for amateur performances of "Cupid Rampant". I also wrote for a number of periodicals over the years, for most of which I received modest fees. Whether paid or not, it was always a pleasure to commit my comments to paper. They stimulated for me the valued friendship of people in many parts of the world for which I have been very grateful.

Stage Lighting Development

I have purposely refrained from examining the remarkable developments of stage lighting practice and the new inventions intended to aid that progress. I could not compete with Fred Bentham, who required 350 pages to do so in the second edition of his book, "The Art of Stage Lighting", published in 1976. The quality and variety of equipment has expanded enormously during the existence of the Manchester Branch, whose activities have inevitably been affected. The equipment provided even for the smallest of stages has become much more extensive and flexible. The contribution of lighting to theatrical production has significantly improved but the quality has been increasingly dependent on the artistry of the responsible personnel. It is now quite customary for "lighting designer" to be nominated in the programme.

There is a tendency for technicians in the theatre, as elsewhere, to become more concerned with the operational "efficiency" of technology than with the quality of results produced. I recollect that on one occasion when an artist friend had been booked to lecture at a meeting of Illuminating Engineers in Manchester but could not appear, I was bullied into taking his place. I decided to assume the attitude of an artist and to make a provocative protest against the misuse of modern lighting. Most of the audience were involved in the use of what were the new types of fluorescent, mercury vapour and sodium lighting, then even more repulsive in their colour distortion than at present. I emphasised the aesthetic importance of colour values in all circumstances and accused them of environmental vandalism. To counter the storm of criticism which ensued I asserted that they wouldn't dare install sodium lighting in the Mall because it would debase the environs of Buckingham Palace so why the devil should they dare to put it outside my house? My forcible exaggerations had sufficient truth to induce quite a lot of uneasy fun and the meeting lasted half an hour longer than usual, without any practical result, of course.

Varied Activities

Perhaps I could be allowed to record some of my varied activities in the course of my service to the theatre. Over the years I was intimately associated with many different organisations, including:

Stockport Garrick Society. I became a member in 1915, became its President in 1959/60 and I continued to act and direct occasionally until I was over 80. I am now an Honorary Life Member.

Association of British Theatre Technicians and **Society of Theatre Consultants.** I was one of the founder members of both and was made Honorary Life Member of each after my retirement.

Society for Theatre Research. I was a member and for several years was Chairman of the Manchester Section.

Illuminating Engineering Society. A member of the Manchester Centre for many years and Chairman for one year; lectured at several centres and attended conferences and dinners in London and various provincial cities.

Theatrical Traders Association. Member of the National Committee in London.

Woodstock, Bramhall Lane, Stockport - the Corry home 1945-1960

PART SEVEN
Retirement

In 1965 at the age of 71 I decided it was time to relinquish the responsibility of managing Watts & Corry as a part of the Strand Electric group. I retired at the end of September, after which I worked intermittently as a Theatre Consultant from an office in my home. I also continued to write for TABS and other journals.

Fred Bentham recorded my retirement under the playful title of "Back to Methuselah", which article I reproduce not solely for its soothing massage of my ego. For more than forty years there has been a unique community spirit between us and it is fitting that he should make a personal contribution to this potted history.

Our provocative styles in exercising our own brands of humour have been curiously complementary. We share hilarious memories, possibly of pontificating on platforms or, maybe, of posing as pundits on a radio programme for which a private rehearsal once collapsed in hilarious self-criticism: also, on a visit to America, of plagiarising for our own amusement some of the more extravagant native pomposities.

During our years of proprietary concern for TABS I observed with approval Fred's outstanding progress from earnest essayist to fluent writer whose serious intent could be decorated by irreverent comment. Gratefully I accepted on retirement what could be regarded as his premature rehearsal for an obituary which, alas, I shall not be able to savour unless it could be one of those undreamed of things in heaven and earth of which Hamlet warned Horatio.

Extract from TABS Volume 23 December 1965

"BACK TO METHUSELAH
by F P Bentham

By the time this is published, a stalwart of TABS will have retired, though not as a contributor to these pages. Percy Corry, at the age of seventy-one, has decided that the Strand Electric will have to do without him in the front line of action. To pay tribute to Percy Corry is a formality for he is well known as himself on account of his world-wide lecturing and extensive writing on theatre subjects. No back-room boy this!

Corry is not only a prolific writer but also a prolific reader and was, as he says, mainly educated at the Public Library, Stockport, having had to sacrifice two years of a scholarship by leaving school at fourteen to augment his "respectable" working-class family's income. In the first world war he enlisted in the Army Service Corps as a driver - of horses and mules. In spite of this it became, shortly after, Royal (R.A.S.C) and more predictably Corry became a Sergeant, the better to employ his pen.

After the war as a manufacturer's agent for confectionery he became an ex-soldier in chocolate-creams. As a disciple of Bernard Shaw, he has carried his devotion to extreme lengths: on the one

Lorcan Bourke, Phil Cantlich, Mary Whitter and Kevin Bourke cheerfully celebrating the Corry retirement in 1965

Jack Madre, Blanche Avison and "Woody" at the Corry retirement party in 1965

hand digesting and keeping down mountains of raw vegetarian bounty, on the other digesting and giving forth the mammoth well-cooked broadsides of the plays. Percy Corry has played most of the big parts, Tanner, Don Juan, Magnus and Shotover. Nevertheless, he has not confined himself thereto, one of his favourite roles being Maurice Meister in Edgar Wallace's "The Ringer" and his most recent role only last year, was Shylock for the Stockport Garrick, with which he has a long association. He states that this Shylock was a Corry version which some approved but others did not. It did not conform to the usual interpretation and he says that, judging it objectively, he feels it was psychologically right but theatrically less effective than he had hoped.

He first began producing in 1924 with "Paolo and Francesca" and has directed scores of plays since, including many of those of the master. It is this role of actor and producer that has made Percy's work for the theatre, particularly the amateur theatre, so valuable. Strand Electric prides itself on knowing intimately the needs of its customers, acting the consultant rather than the salesman. Strand Electric itself, of course, knows nothing: it is the individuals it attracts and has attracted that make it what it is. Of course none was more influential than Corry.

So much for "Superman" (to misunderstand G.B.S). What kind of man is he? Well, certainly two-masked, for he has found no difficulty in playing managing director of his own firm, "Watts & Corry", and founder manager of "Strand Electric", Manchester, at one and the same time. During the Second World War he was able to goad and

Fred Bentham demonstrating, in 1974, his latest system of stage lighting control designed for Stratford on Avon Memorial Theatre

inspire the Torpedo Attack Teacher and other specialised trainers to success by doubling the part of director of the principal contractor and manager of a sub-contractor. With all respect to the others mixed up in this strange wartime adventure it owed everything to Corry's energy.

It should not be assumed that he thrives only in the limelight; for throughout the long years of anonymity imposed by the original editor of TABS, his pen was busy on unsigned contributions or heavily disguised ones as "Busker". Quite why staff contributions had to be anonymous is not at all clear, especially as Corry was one of the two (the other was Applebee) to grace the pre-war pages complete with potted biography and photograph.

By the way, Percy Corry is no longer a vegetarian; too true to be good, he was nearly as flexible in this respect as the stage installations he planned. Some will regard this as a sad tale of decline and fall; others will see it as the wisdom that goes with age."

Robbie's Retirement

In March of the same year Robbie retired at the age of 60. She was needed at home as her mother was approaching 90. After my retirement we were able to maintain our friendship and shared many holidays together.

One of the penalties of a long life is the loss of so many relatives and friends. As already reported my wife died in 1960. My mother died in 1954 at the age of 88. At various intervals, I have lost by death both sisters, four sisters-in-law and four brothers-in-law (Edgar still survives at the age of 91). Robbie's mother died some years ago at an age of well over 90 and in August 1982 Robbie herself, then at the age of 77, died very suddenly.

Kenneth Greaves, Marjorie Robinson and author in celebratory mood

EPILOGUE
Take-over by Rank Organisation

Early in 1968 Rank made an offer for Strand Electric (which was a public limited company) but this was rejected by the shareholders. Rank, with rather reckless optimism, then increased their bid, which was accepted. Strand thus became an addition to their Audio-Visual Group and its administration was re-organised to conform to the more "sophisticated" pattern favoured by managerial personnel.

The name Watts & Corry was dropped in favour of Rank Strand Electric. A new General Manager for the Manchester organisation was imported from one of the other subsidiaries but he was not an outstanding success and soon disappeared. The Gorton premises were sold (profitably, no doubt) and the personnel transferred to a factory occupied by another firm in the Group, situated at Lowton, between Manchester and Liverpool. This was not easily accessible to those of the staff who lacked cars, my son included, and they left the company.

The TV Scenery Section, although operating very profitably, was sold by Rank to the Trident Group which controlled both Yorkshire and Tyne-Tees Television companies and the name Watts & Corry Ltd was immediately restored. The bakery building proved to be too small and they moved in due course to more commodious premises. In the meantime, Stuart Avison resigned and became Manager of the Scenery Department of the Granada Studios in Manchester.

Rank lost many other former Strand employees in London and elsewhere owing to death, resignation or retirement, including all who were directors when the take-over occurred. Fred Bentham opted for early retirement in 1973 when it was decided to change the policy and format of TABS which had been his main concern for many years. I shared disapproval of the change of size to A4. The original size was conveniently handy and fitted perfectly into the bookcase when bound. My collection has been invaluable in prompting memories of the past. Since his own retirement he has edited a quarterly journal of similar size and style to the old TABS, issued by the A.B.T.T, entitled "Sightline". It has a pronounced technical emphasis.

It is quite interesting that one section of the expanded firm created by Humphrey Watts has travelled full circle despite the changes of ownership. There is an affinity with Fitups, whose original primary purpose was the supply of scenery. It is quite gratifying to see the large vans of Watts & Corry passing through the environs of Manchester periodically.

After my retirement I established an office at my home address and operated as an independent Theatre Consultant. I continued to write and to lecture for several years but early in 1981 I suffered a mild stroke which has restricted my mobility: this can be very frustrating. I now regard my active working life as completed. It has lasted for some 75 years and has, I hope, justified my existence to some extent.

There is not a lot to be said in favour of old age but one can be grateful for the affection and consideration shown by the many friends acquired during the years. Particularly do I value the good fellowship of those younger associates whose progress from eager youth to seasoned maturity I have observed with some slightly paternal concern. It is very satisfying to find that they can still accept me with goodwill and without any indication that allowance is being made for senility that age gaps might suggest.

I have lived during the reigns of six different monarchs, one of whom - Edward the Eighth - abdicated before being crowned. I listened to his farewell speech broadcast on what was then the "Home Service". I suspected that his unspoken sentiment could have been "For this relief much thanks". His brother had to relinquish the dukedom of York to become George the Sixth. It was, I think, a change of Kings for the better and it gave the British people a Queen who earned a unique affection which caused the universal granting to her of the unofficial title of "Queen Mum". During my lifetime we have had more prime ministers than I need to recall individually. Perhaps the most colourful and most eloquent was Lloyd George who, before becoming premier, was mainly responsible for the National Insurance Act of 1911 which was an initial attempt to establish rather tentatively something like a "Welfare State", ultimately developed by Beveridge after the first of the wars intended, it was often claimed (rather foolishly) to be the war to end all war.

In these days if I am prepared to declare my political convictions I am tempted to describe myself as a disillusioned democrat. I have occasionally revived memories of early enthusiasm for socialistic principles which make me tolerant of young people who are similarly convinced that our society could be successfully reorganised to remove the inequalities that are so obvious. Having observed the failure of so many attempts in various parts of the world I have become convinced that the fault lies not in the organisation of society so much as in the basic failure of the human race to recognise the needs of collectivism and to renounce the selfish ambitions of individuals. If all the nations which profess to believe in the principles of Christianity, for example, and of other religions were willing to accept and act on those principles instead of finding excuses for deviations there would not be any need to strive for reorganisation. The Crusaders tried to justify the cross with which they decorated their armour by calling "infidels" those whom they slaughtered in "defence" of Christendom.

Most of the Western nations can be eloquent in paying lip service to Democracy but will pay cash extravagantly to induce professional advertisers to convince the gullible voters that black is not quite black but is some colour that can be manipulated to appear more attractive. There are innumerable conferences of international specialists in every walk of life claiming to seek co-operation for the general good, but each striving to get the maximum benefit for their own countries or organisations at the expense of the rest.

It becomes painfully obvious that the whole business of organising communal life has become too complex for the rulers and would-be rulers to avoid ensuring that the human race is heading for self-destruction. Perhaps one is being too pessimistic: perhaps miracles are still possible, if they ever were! There is much good intent in